"Wherever you are in your journey of learning about and  *The Antiracism Handbook* will help you move ahead with clarity, co... and your fellow travelers. Grounded in psychological research and i... ...ience, it is a much-needed resource for anyone—White or BIPOC—wh... ...ome more effective in interrupting the cycle of racism. Use it yourself and share it with others!"

> —**Beverly Daniel Tatum, PhD**, *New York Times* bestselling author of *Why Are All the Black Kids Sitting Together in the Cafeteria?*

"A must-read for mental health professionals, this cutting-edge masterwork from two acclaimed therapist/scholars pairs clinical strategies with targeted exercises to provide *current* navigation of the challenges in becoming an effective antiracist advocate. Thema Bryant and Edith Arrington demonstrate that cultivating antiracism is a significant step in the creation of a just and equitable society—and *show you how*. I highly recommend this excellent handbook!"

> —**Lillian Comas-Díaz, PhD**, clinical professor in the department of psychiatry and behavioral sciences at George Washington University, and author of *Multicultural Care*

"*The Antiracism Handbook* is an urgent invitation to confront the truth about race and racism, and build the capabilities needed to do the work of racial justice in our lives and society. Drawing from resources in mindfulness and cognitive behavioral therapy (CBT)—as well as liberatory, decolonial, and community psychology—the authors expertly guide readers through a curriculum that requires active participation: rigorous self-examination, truth-telling, deep learning and unlearning, identifying barriers, and skill building. Eradicating racism will take all of us. Practitioners everywhere should read this book, which is sure to become required reading in the years ahead."

> —**Tabatha L. Jones Jolivet, PhD**, associate professor of higher education at Azusa Pacific University, community organizer, and coauthor of *White Jesus*

"Thema Bryant and Edith Arrington bring wisdom, compassion, and extensive knowledge to this excellent handbook. The reflection exercises, mindfulness moments, practical recommendations, and selection of topics are powerful offerings for both white and BIPOC readers to participate meaningfully in the work of antiracism. They accompany you with a presence of deep care and inspired commitment to healing the individual and collective damage of systemic racism. Prepare to be transformed!"

> —**Shelly P. Harrell, PhD**, professor of psychology at Pepperdine University, developer of the *Racism and Life Experience Scales*, and founder/director of *The Soulfulness Center*

"*The Antiracism Handbook* is an extraordinarily comprehensive guide for addressing racial inequity. Thema Bryant and Edith Arrington demystify antiracism and expose pervasive barriers to antiracism work while equipping the reader with mindset-shifting activities and behavioral strategies. The book simultaneously challenges and inspires the reader to action. It is a must-read for anyone who is ready to integrate allyship into daily practice, and also for individuals who need respite from unaddressed racism-related fatigue."

> —**Rheeda Walker, PhD**, professor of psychology at the University of Houston, licensed psychologist, and author of *The Unapologetic Guide to Black Mental Health*

The Social Justice Handbook Series

As culture evolves, we need new tools to help us cope and interact with our social world in ways that feel authentic and empowered. That's why New Harbinger created the *Social Justice Handbook* series—a series that teaches readers how to use practical, psychology-based tools to challenge and transform dominant culture, both in their daily lives and in their communities.

Written by thought leaders in the fields of psychology, sociology, gender, and ethnic studies, the *Social Justice Handbook* series offers evidence-based strategies for coping with a broad range of social inequities that impact quality of life. As research has shown us, social oppression can lead to mental health issues such as depression, anxiety, trauma, lowered self-esteem, and self-harm. These handbooks provide accessible social analysis as well as thoughtful activities and exercises based on the latest psychological methods to help readers unlearn internalized negative messages, resist social inequities, transform their communities, and challenge dominant culture to be equitable for all.

The handbooks also serve as a hands-on resource for therapists who wish to integrate an understanding and acknowledgement of how multiple social issues impact their clients to provide relevant and supportive care.

For a complete list of books in
the *Social Justice Handbook* series,
visit newharbinger.com

THE
ANTIRACISM
HANDBOOK

PRACTICAL TOOLS TO SHIFT YOUR MINDSET & UPROOT RACISM IN YOUR LIFE & COMMUNITY

THEMA BRYANT, PHD | EDITH G. ARRINGTON, PHD

New Harbinger Publications, Inc.

Distributed in Canada by Raincoast Books

NEW HARBINGER PUBLICATIONS is a registered trademark of New Harbinger Publications, Inc.

Copyright © 2022 by Thema Bryant-Davis and Edith G. Arrington
        New Harbinger Publications, Inc.
        5674 Shattuck Avenue
        Oakland, CA 94609
        www.newharbinger.com

Cover design by Sara Christian

Acquired by Elizabeth Hollis Hansen

Edited by Teja Watson

All Rights Reserved

Library of Congress Cataloging-in-Publication Data

Names: Bryant-Davis, Thema, author. | Arrington, Edith, author.
Title: The antiracism handbook : practical tools to shift your mindset and uproot racism in your life and
    community / by Thema Bryant-Davis and Edith Arrington, PhD.
Description: Oakland, CA : New Harbinger Publications, [2022] | Series: Social justice handbook |
    Includes bibliographical references.
Identifiers: LCCN 2021038777 | ISBN 9781684039104 (trade paperback)
Subjects: LCSH: Anti-racism. | Racism--Prevention.
Classification: LCC HT1563 .B79 2022 | DDC 305.8--dc23
LC record available at https://lccn.loc.gov/2021038777

Printed in the United States of America

24   23   22

10   9   8   7   6   5   4   3   2   1   First Printing

To our parents, who inspired us to live fully our commitments
to antiracism, liberation, and love in action

Contents

Foreword

Over my past two decades of teaching about social justice issues, it has become very clear that many people have difficulties in talking about race and racism—particularly with people of other racial groups. When the topic of race emerges in classroom settings, a palpable tension often arises. When I've asked about it, some students share that they don't want to say the wrong things or offend others in the room. Other people reveal how their previous negative dialogues about race make them hesitant or weary about engaging in current or future conversations. Some Black, Indigenous, and other people of color (BIPOC) students describe being tired of talking about race (especially with white people) or recognizing the unfair burden of representing entire racial groups. Meanwhile, some white students report feeling a lot of guilt or shame, which limits their ability to fully engage.

Through research and anecdotal experiences, I have learned that the reasons behind these difficult dialogues are not universal. For example, discussing race may be arduous for many white people because they do not typically have conversations about race at all. Scholars like psychologist Helen Neville and sociologist Eduardo Bonilla-Silva have described how white people have been taught to operate from a color-blind racial ideology—or the belief system that race and racism do not exist, that all people have the same opportunities regardless of skin color, and that it is rude or impolite to discuss race with others (along with other topics like politics and religion). So, when asked to reflect and share race-related insights in public settings (e.g., classrooms, workplaces, etc.), many white people are being asked to engage in foreign practices. Accordingly, such conversations result in myriad psychological and emotional reactions including defensiveness, intellectualization, anger, or overwhelming guilt.

Conversely, some people of color may think about race all time, but have difficulty discussing it with others—out of fear of being pathologized, misunderstood, invalidated, or even punished. Indeed, extensive scholarship has supported that BIPOCs think (and talk) about race quite often. Foundational research by psychologists like William Cross, Janet Helms, Derald Wing Sue, and Thomas Parham has highlighted how BIPOCs navigate the world based on their racial identities. Other psychologists, such as Diane Hughes and Howard Stevenson, have described the process of racial socialization—or the ways BIPOC parents (especially Black American parents) may prepare their children for the racism they are expected to face in the world. Further, psychologists Thema Bryant, Lillian Comas-Díaz, and Robert Carter have written about racial trauma—the significant psychological distress resulting from personal accumulative experiences with systemic racism, racial discrimination, and microaggressions as well as communities' collective and historical connections with racial violence. So, while many BIPOC may be viscerally aware of the role of race and racism in their lives (and are generally well-equipped to talk about racism on both cognitive and emotional levels), such conversations with people who have limited knowledge of racial issues are often accompanied by fears of retraumatization, stigmatization, and more.

When people cannot talk about race or racism, it is significantly more challenging to talk about antiracism—or the intentional commitment through which people, communities, and institutions actively combat racism, internally, interpersonally, and systemically. While some people are intellectually interested or invested in navigating against racism, they may not know where to start, nor have the tools to do so. They might also have difficulty connecting emotionally or lack the capacity to integrate antiracist principles into all aspects of their lives.

It is for these reasons that *The Antiracism Handbook: Practical Tools to Shift Your Mindset and Uproot Racism in Your Life and Community* by Drs. Thema Bryant and Edith Arrington is a necessary text for people who are interested in becoming, or maintaining their identities as, antiracist advocates. In the first part, the authors provide a poignant overview of how racism has infiltrated every part of what is now known as the United States while encouraging self-reflections on race and racial identity, intersectional identities, power, and privilege. They push readers to hold themselves accountable to learning (or unlearning) all the messages they have acquired about race and racism. For white people, this includes challenging notions about equity and meritocracy; for BIPOC, the focus may be on identifying and disrupting the many harmful messages they have internalized about their racial groups.

The second part of the workbook critically highlights the many internal defenses that prohibit people from genuinely engaging in antiracist work—ranging from guilt to avoidance to biases. While such emotional processes differ for people of various racial groups, core commonalities can prevent people from engaging in real antiracist practices. Naming and normalizing these challenges are crucial; without doing so, it becomes easier for people to sit in complacency or to minimize the urgency of obliterating oppression.

The last parts of the handbook describe useful strategies for engaging in antiracist principles; practice exercises give readers the preparation necessary for if or when they find themselves in problematic race-related situations. In a similar way that people should know what to do in emergency situations (e.g., fires, earthquakes, etc.), it's also beneficial to brainstorm how to respond to awkward, anxiety-provoking, microaggressive situations. Further, the authors name additional burdens of practicing antiracism, from racial battle fatigue to activist burnout. They end with strategies on how to sustain oneself as an antiracist advocate—reminding readers of their sacred purposes and the need for holistically taking care of one's body, heart, mind, culture, and spirit.

The *Antiracism Handbook* is a must-read for people interested in combating racism—from those dipping their toes in social justice activism to long-term activists who have been on the front lines for decades. Drs. Bryant and Arrington should be commended for presenting a breadth of material in such palpable and accessible ways. If people authentically engaged in the workbook's various reflection exercises throughout the duration of their lives, perhaps dialogues about race and racism would be less difficult. And if every person committed to this lifelong learning, our society would (or could) take the first step toward truly advocating for equity and justice.

—Kevin L. Nadal, PhD
City University of New York

Beginning Our Work Together to Cultivate Antiracism

This workbook came to fruition in the spring and summer of 2020. One of us, Thema, had developed a presentation on "Moving from Cultural Competence to Antiracism" earlier that year and was asked to consider diving deeper into the topic by writing a workbook that would expand and explore the ways in which people could approach antiracism consistently and authentically in their work (for those in the mental health arena) or in their lives more broadly. Thema reached out to her friend and colleague, Edith, to see if she would be interested in writing the workbook together given Edith's work exploring race, racial identity, and racism in K-12 schools, communities, and nonprofit organizations.

Under ordinary circumstances, as Black women psychologists, we would have been thrilled to work and write together on a topic that has been meaningful to us throughout our lives—from childhood through our professional careers. But the spring and summer of 2020 were certainly not ordinary. And the commitment to writing this workbook became even more important to us as a way to contribute to the necessary work being done to address our nation's (long overdue) racial reckoning.

Breonna Taylor was shot eight times while sleeping in her home in Louisville, KY. Ahmaud Arbery was shot and killed while out jogging in suburban Atlanta. George Floyd's life was taken from him over the extended length of time that a police officer lodged his knee on Mr. Floyd's neck. In all of those instances, and in too many others, we were reminded of how precarious Black lives are in our society. Additionally, in the months prior to George Floyd's murder, we were witness to a growing number of people dying from a global pandemic that was disproportionately impacting Black people, Indigenous people, and people of color (BIPOC). By late May 2020, the number of deaths from COVID-19 totaled 100,000 and deaths continued to rise through the summer to cross the 200,000 mark. The reality of the lives we lost was the backdrop to what seemed to be a never-ending loop of news stories and videos of Black lives being taken through state-sanctioned violence.

The protests that arose over Memorial Day weekend that year were somehow different from protests in the past. It may have been that protests were taking place simultaneously across the country, from urban centers to the suburbs to rural areas. It might also have been seeing the diverse races, genders, and ages of the people that joined the Black community to proclaim that "Black Lives Matter." Whatever it was that felt different, it was striking to see such a broad acknowledgment that all was not well and that systemic racism is itself a longstanding pandemic that shapes the reality and lives not only of BIPOC but White people as well.

The racial reckoning our nation was experiencing acknowledged systemic racism in contemporary and historical American society and the central role played by the legacy of anti-Blackness in our society. All of a sudden, "Black Lives Matter" could be seen and heard on TV, social media, advertising, yard signs, and painted across the width of streets across the country. Corporations and institutions of higher learning vowed to stand with the Black community and examine their policies and practices to ensure they were equitable. The *New York Times* Bestseller list was filled with books that addressed racism and antiracism. While heartening to some extent, and most certainly belated in any respect, we were left to wonder: what did it all mean for how people could actually address racism and bring about change?

This question is what motivated us to develop this workbook. We wanted to explore how each of us can better understand race and racism in order to enact antiracism—purposeful, committed action to combat racism in all the ways it is expressed—in our lives, relationships, and communities. This is important because we are working toward not only health as individuals and in our communities but also to achieve racial equity, justice, and liberation across all aspects of American society—and the world. And we believe that the way we'll get there is by every one of us working to cultivate antiracism in our lives and communities.

When we talk about *antiracism*, we mean the ways in which individuals, communities, and organizations can actively counter racism across the multiple levels—interpersonal, cultural, institutional, and internalized—that it is expressed.

WHY THIS HANDBOOK? AND HOW WILL IT WORK?

Now that we've described how this handbook came to fruition, we want to say more about what we hope it accomplishes for you (and for us). When we say "Black Lives Matter," we are affirming the humanity of Black people, knowing that the racism and colonialism prevalent throughout American history threaten the lives and health of Black people. We also acknowledge that the discrimination, state violence, and restricted economic access (to affordable housing, well-paying work, health care, and much more) that result from America's history of racism profoundly affect Black people—as well as Indigenous people and other people of color. And racism has consequences for White Americans too, as professor of sociology Jonathan Metzl (2019) describes in his book *Dying of Whiteness*. As Metzl notes, the more racial resentment White people felt, the more likely they were to endorse policies that restrict access to health care or make it easier to obtain guns—both of which increase mortality.

So, as you can see, race and racism matter for everyone. And while we are glad that more people are paying attention to the numerous stories in the news and on social media, we want to make it clear: *Race and racism are not new*. And neither is the antiracist work that members of the BIPOC and White communities have been doing for a long time now.

As psychologists, we have spent the last twenty years of our careers committed to improving the health of individuals and communities (with a particular focus on the Black community and other people of color), through our clinical, research, teaching, consulting, and advocacy efforts. Underlying all the facets of our work is the aim to better understand the dynamics and impact of race and racism.

Thema is the daughter of African Methodist Episcopal (AME) ministers who lived and worked in the Black community in Baltimore. Edith's parents were Black educators in suburban New York, where she grew up. Both of our parents were committed to the Black community; in the church, community, and educational settings, they advanced Black history and culture through courses, books, and other resources they advocated for students to have access to. Our parents knew racial socialization was critical to raising Black children who loved themselves, their families, and the broader Black community. As a result, both of us were supported by a positive *racial identity*, a positive sense of ourselves, as Black people, as we grew up. And in adulthood, we've built upon this foundation of positive racial identity through our commitment to using psychology to better understand race and confront racism so that our community can be as healthy as possible.

Our approach to using psychology to promote health is grounded in the awareness that individual health alone is not sufficient. How we live in connection to others and our communities is vital to being as healthy as possible. We believe that racism, oppression, and colonization are threats to health—not in an abstract way, but in tangible ways that impact us every day such as whether we live in neighborhoods that are racially segregated or under-resourced, whether we have access to quality health care, or whether we report higher levels of stress in our lives (Williams, Lawrence, and Davis 2019).

So, in this book, we will explore how insights from cognitive behavioral therapy, mindfulness, liberation and decolonizing psychology, and community psychology can be used to support you to engage in the work of antiracism right now and to sustain this work for a lifetime, in your own life, and in your community.

First, we'll reflect on race—what it is, how we learn about ourselves as members of racial groups, and how and what we learn about the role race plays in inequality and oppression throughout our society. We'll also explore how we can educate ourselves about race and racism and what roles power and privilege play in how we experience them.

Then, we'll tackle the various barriers that can make it hard for us to cope with, and in some cases accept, the reality of racism, and work to combat it in our lives and societies. Those barriers include avoiding addressing race and racism, feeling guilt for racism (which is understandable, but usually unproductive), being unaware of the realities of race and racism, and fear—for instance, that you'll be punished for speaking out, or that confronting racism will be uncomfortable in ways you're not sure you can handle.

Finally, we'll discuss concrete ways to cultivate an antiracist life: how you can be antiracist across different interpersonal settings, advocate for antiracist policies and practices, raise your children to be antiracist, and practice antiracism in sacred spaces like your church.

We know this work will not be easy. You'll inevitably encounter pushback as you challenge racism in your life. For some of us, this struggle has been ongoing. For others, the pushback may be new, especially if you've never challenged racism before. Either way, it is natural to feel fatigued or be discouraged. So, we'll also work to build your resources for the inevitable points of struggle and pain in your antiracist journey: helping you recognize when you're fatigued or discouraged and when you need to practice self-care and seek support from your community. We want you to be able to keep the faith as you continue doing the work so you're as healthy as possible as you sustain your antiracism efforts.

Please note that there are free tools that accompany this book: worksheets for various activities in the book, two bonus chapters, and a reading group guide for those who might choose to read this book as part of a group or club. These tools are available at http://www.newharbinger.com/49104.

SO, WHY ARE YOU HERE?

We imagine that you were drawn to this handbook because you experienced some sort of shock or jolt or increase in intensity around how you *feel* and *think* about race and racism. You may have had (or witnessed) an experience at work, school, or in your community that made you *feel* sad, angry, scared, frustrated, and/or guilty about racial injustice and racism. Or perhaps you have become more aware of racial injustice and racism through lived experience, watching the news, or reading social media, blogs, articles, and/or books that shifted the way you *think* about yourself, your relationships, and your community, and perhaps how you think about others. And now, you want to *do something* in response. Maybe you recognize that you need to learn more about race and racism. Or you want to change a policy or practice you see in your community that you believe is unjust. Or you witnessed racist behavior taking place in the past and you didn't know what to do then, but you want to know what to do the next time something similar happens. We hope this handbook will offer you strategies for enacting antiracism in meaningful ways in your life.

We'll note here that we expect our readers to be BIPOC *and* White. Members from both of these broad communities have a vested interest in ending racism, and everyone in these groups has a role to play in that work. Given the way that race is lived and racism is experienced within and across diverse communities, you'll likely come to this workbook with your own levels of experience and comfort in talking about race and racism. That's fine and to be expected.

If you're a BIPOC reader, you might need to: explore and unlearn some internalized patterns of thought or behavior that years of living with racism have instilled in you; affirm your sense of yourself and your pride in your racial identity; and learn skills to advocate for yourself and others. You might also need to confront some privileges you have, too, depending on which BIPOC group you're a part of. We hope that what you take away from this handbook is a set of strategies that strengthen your mind, body, and spirit to allow you to continue to confront the impact racism has had on your life and stay engaged in antiracist work on your own behalf and on behalf of others.

For our White readers, your experience in grappling with race and confronting racism may fall anywhere across a wide range: some of you may have limited experience dealing with race and acknowledging racism, but you're willing to learn more; others among you may already be engaged in ongoing work as an ally in our collective struggle for liberation. Your task in this handbook will include coming to grips with your privilege—and with the indifference and egotism that can come with it—so you can cultivate and strengthen your commitment to living an antiracist life.

Ultimately, wherever you are in the antiracism journey, all we ask is that you stay invested, interrogate racism as you encounter it in the world around you, and commit to taking steps to change it.

REFLECTION EXERCISE: Why Are You Here?

Take a moment now to reflect on why you picked up this handbook. Write your answers in the space provided below.

What motivated you to pick up this book? Was it a personal experience you had or witnessed? Something you read in the news or on social media? Saw on TV?

_____

_____

_____

If it was because of an experience, how were you feeling? Be specific; name the emotions.

_____

_____

_____

What were you thinking? Did you realize or learn anything new?

_____

_____

_____

Now that you have this handbook, what do you hope will happen next? What goal(s) do you want to achieve by the end of your journey with us?

_____

_____

_____

As you move through the book, please keep your motivation for starting this work in mind, and reflect on it periodically. We hope it will help sustain you when your attention, commitment, or energy wavers—which is to be expected. Facing race and confronting racism can be emotionally, spiritually, and physically challenging. But it is necessary if you want to cultivate antiracism as authentically and consistently as possible.

We want you to prepare yourself for this journey in which you'll think critically and carefully, be honest with yourself, and stay open to self-reflection. We'll also provide you with some tools to guide you along the way. There will be a number of written reflection exercises and embodied healing exercises. We will also present a series of Mindful Moments as opportunities for you to reflect on a new concept or take a step back and check in with yourself.

As Vice President Kamala Harris said when she accepted the nomination as vice president for the Democratic Party: "There is no vaccine for systemic racism. You have to do the work." So, let's begin this work together: committing to facing race, confronting racism, and cultivating antiracism.

PART 1

Laying the Foundation for Antiracism

In this first part of the *Antiracism Handbook*, we begin by laying the foundation to better understanding and working toward antiracism. We'll explore race and racism in a more in-depth way by focusing on how we learn and talk about race and how we understand ourselves in relation to race and racism. Then, we'll explore how we can educate ourselves and also take a closer look at just what we mean by *power* and *privilege*.

The foundations of the first part of the handbook will help us set the stage for the second part, where we'll discuss some of the barriers to cultivating antiracism in our personal relationships, professional roles and through civic engagement and advocacy. Let's get started.

CHAPTER 1

Reflecting on Race and Racism as the First Steps to Antiracism

The highly publicized deaths of Black men, women, and children over the past several years, along with the disproportionate impact of COVID-19 on many communities of color, have brightened the spotlight on the systemic and insidious ways in which racism manifests. While all of us have been impacted by systemic racism, some of us have been disadvantaged directly, where others with more privilege have been affected more indirectly, and in some cases have been advantaged. And some of us have been affected over a sustained period of time while others may have encountered systemic racism that was easy to ignore or rationalize away. When, for whatever reason, you come to see more clearly the racial injustice that exists or encounter it through direct experience, it can motivate you to do something to make a difference whether you're BIPOC or White. We think you chose to pick up this book because you want to commit to working toward antiracism.

By "antiracism," we mean actively and intentionally working to counter racism across the many levels in which it can manifest. We will dive deeper into the levels of racism later in this chapter, but will take time now to clarify that racism can be experienced interpersonally, culturally, and institutionally. As such, your antiracist work may take place in personal spheres of your life such as at work or home. Maybe you decide to stand up for a colleague who's being discriminated against, or defend family members against the invective of a racist family member. Your antiracist work may target systems, as you invest your time and energy in changing unjust social policies that disproportionately impact communities of color.

Because there is such a wide range of contexts in which you can engage in this work, it may feel overwhelming to think about how you will go about cultivating antiracism or being an antiracist. This is especially the case if you've generally avoided talking or thinking about race, or if you tend to view racism as isolated, extreme acts of prejudice or discrimination against others, or as something firmly in America's past rather than something that can and does happen all the time, in both extreme and seemingly mundane ways.

In this chapter, we'll challenge assumptions like these by looking at what we must face in order to be antiracist: what race and racism are and how they affect our identities as well as our society. We hope this process of reflection will prepare you to tackle various barriers like avoidance, guilt, and indifference, which can make it hard to act in antiracist ways—especially if you are White or otherwise privileged. By the end of this chapter, you'll be better informed about race and racism and more prepared to tackle these barriers.

A CLOSER LOOK: THE REALITY OF RACE

You may have heard that race is not real. That's not quite accurate. Race is real in that it directly affects our lives. Since humans are social beings who live in relation to one another, race has meaning as a social construct. However, race is *not* a valid biological construct as there are many more similarities and only a minute (less than 1 percent) genetic variation between members of different racial groups (Smedley and Smedley 2005). Pieterse and Powell (2016, 12) define race as "a system of social categorization based on skin color and physical features."

In the United States, racial groups currently counted in the United States Census include: American Indian or Alaska Native, Asian, Black or African American, Native Hawaiian or other Pacific Islander, and White. Only some of these racial groups are indigenous to the North American continent; many of us came instead from various regions of the world via immigration (traveling to and settling in a new country), enslavement (as with African people forcibly brought to America to exploit their labor), and colonization (the process by which, historically, nations in Europe established colonies, often displacing people in those countries). Although Latinx is considered an ethnic group (which shares cultural markers such as language) and not a racial group, they have been racialized to the extent that they have experienced disadvantages as compared to non-Latinx White people. It is important to note that Latinxs may also be a member of one or more racial groups (for example, Afro-Latinxs). Additionally, people who are Middle Eastern and North African (MENA) have advocated recently to not default to the White category given they have been racialized in ways that do not reflect the advantages of Whiteness.

How a society understands, perceives, and treats people from different racial groups has very real impacts on people's growth, development, relationships, health, and overall quality of life. Understanding these impacts means exploring what race means on the individual level—your *racial identity*—and the societal level, or the *racial hierarchy* through which various racial groups are valued.

Let's look more closely at the racial hierarchy: how it operates on a societal level and shapes our lived experience of racial identity.

The Racial Hierarchy

In the racial hierarchy, the forces of White supremacy and anti-Blackness* create a system where Whiteness is the most valued or advantaged social status, and Blackness is the most devalued and disadvantaged. Other racial groups occupy a disadvantaged status relative to those who are White or more advantaged, relative to those who are Black.

The racial hierarchy shapes how people from different racial groups navigate race in our society. If you're part of a group with a higher-status level in the racial hierarchy, you probably have more say in the racial dynamics at play in any given situation and you may be more able to choose whether you want to engage with race or not. If you're part of a racial group that's devalued and disadvantaged in the racial hierarchy, you probably don't have the luxury of choosing to engage with race or deciding whether you will acknowledge its existence.

This is because the levels of power and privilege assigned within the racial hierarchy have been codified into policies and laws throughout American history, which impact our day-to-day social interactions. Members of groups disadvantaged in the racial hierarchy may encounter everyday experiences of racial slights (also known as microaggressions), or they might experience discrimination that limits access to housing or health care or job opportunities, or be disproportionately targeted by law enforcement.

> *What do you mean by "White supremacy"? And "anti-Blackness"?*
>
> When we refer to **White supremacy**, we mean the cultural, economic, and political system where Whiteness is maintained at the top of the racial hierarchy through the reproduction and reinforcement of ideas that affirm White superiority and the inferiority of other racial groups (Grzanka, Gonzalez, and Spanierman 2019).
>
> **Anti-Blackness** is anti-Black bias built on deep-seated beliefs disregarding the full humanity of Black people (Pearman 2020; Ross 2020).

Laws and policies reinforcing the American racial hierarchy became more stringent after twenty Africans arrived in Virginia in 1619, and have had incredible consequences on how race has been lived in our country over the last four hundred years (Wilkerson 2020).

RACIAL HISTORY AND HIERARCHY IN THE UNITED STATES

How much do you know about race and our nation's history? We may have learned about some of the major periods and events in America's past—such as slavery or the genocide of America's

Indigenous people—but hardly all of them, and often not in much detail. Take a moment now to test your knowledge of the policies and laws that have created and reinforced America's racial hierarchy over time:

1. The Trail of Tears, where Native Americans were forcibly removed from their land in the Southeastern United States and made to walk hundreds of miles to the west, was a result of the Indian Removal Act signed into law by President Andrew Jackson in 1830.

    True   False

2. Until the passage of the Thirteen and Fourteenth Amendments, the United States Constitution declared that Black people were three-fifths of a person.

    True   False

3. In 1947, the ruling by the Ninth Circuit Court of Appeals in *Mendez v. Westminster School District,* in favor of Mexican American families who sued California school districts who blocked them from receiving a quality education, served as a precedent for the Supreme Court's *Brown v. Board of Education* ruling, which outlawed segregation in schools.

    True   False

4. More than 100,000 Japanese-Americans were interned in camps in the Western United States during World War II as a result of a federal order by President Franklin Delano Roosevelt.

    True   False

5. The vast majority of states had laws that made interracial marriage illegal until a Supreme Court ruling in the 1960s.

    True   False

Answer Key: All of the above statements are true. Over the course of history, these policies and laws have had real consequences on BIPOC and White people including how and where they live, love, learn, and work.

We encourage you to explore more of the historical aspects of race and racism in our country on your own by seeking out books, podcasts, and lectures about race and antiracism from historians and social scientists.

Let's consider another dimension to the ways you might understand yourself as a racial being: where the racial group you're a part of—or groups, if you're multiracial—stands in the racial hierarchy.

On Racial Identity

Your *racial identity* refers both to how important race is to your sense of self and the particular meaning you make of your racial group membership(s) (Sellers et al. 1998). Again, even if the racial hierarchy makes it seem as though race is something only BIPOC have, while White people are somehow exempt, we all have a racial identity and we all need to acknowledge the influence our race has on our lives and the lives of others. It's crucial to resist this line of thinking, which so often allows those of us who are White to say they are "color-blind"—after all, if they "don't have" a race themselves, then they can claim not to see it in others, which means discounting a key aspect of someone else's identity while still gaining advantages from being higher status in the racial hierarchy.

Racial identity theories explode this myth of color-blindness while providing helpful frameworks for understanding the meaning of race in our lives. As you'll discover, if we can understand what race and racism mean in our lives and the lives of those around us, we're better able to see ourselves and others in honest, healthy, and affirming ways, and work toward an antiracist society that's fair for all.

William Cross (1991) and Janet Helms (1990) are psychologists who have done trailblazing research and theorizing on racial identity for BIPOC and White people. Their theories on racial identity describe how individuals move from becoming aware that they belong to specific racial groups to developing a sense of meaning about their race that fosters psychological health and positive engagement with people from their and other racial groups. Other psychologists have explored racial identity as a multidimensional concept that addresses how important race is to a person; how a person feels about their racial group; how a person thinks others view their racial group; how a person believes members of their racial group should act; and how salient racial identity is to a person in various settings—or the idea that your racial identity can be more or less meaningful to you in different situations, which can influence how you respond in those situations (Sellers et al. 1998).

Take a moment to reflect on your racial identity by responding to the questions below.

Of which racial group(s) are you a member?

_____

_____

How does it make you feel to be a member of your racial group(s)? How important is it to you to be a member of your racial group(s)?

_____

_____

_____

How do you think other people view or feel about your racial group(s)?

_____

_____

Think back on the situations when being a member of your racial group(s) was particularly salient to you, perhaps a family gathering or get-together with friends. Or it may have been a more stressful event. What was happening? How did you feel? What were you thinking?

_____

_____

_____

We hope that as you reflected on your answers to these questions, you gained insight into how you currently understand and feel about your racial identity. Perhaps you also noticed how much of your experience of racial identity is influenced by the ways you relate to others—through a process known as *racial socialization*.

Racial Socialization and Literacy

Racial socialization is the way in which we learn about race and membership in our racial group(s). Research explores how Black families and other families of color aim to foster a positive racial identity for their children and prepare them for any racism they may confront. There is a much less robust (but growing) body of research on racial socialization strategies for White families (Bartoli et al. 2016), which reflects their ability to not have to engage with race and its impact as often as those who are disadvantaged in the hierarchy do.

Related to racial socialization is *racial literacy*, or your ability to understand race and its role in inequality and oppression (Horsford 2014). Racial literacy can also help you develop coping skills to navigate racially stressful encounters. By considering your own racial socialization and literacy, you'll be better able to understand your racial identity and use it as a resource to confront internal and external roadblocks to living and acting in antiracist ways. We believe your antiracist work will be authentic and affirming if you're well-grounded in where you've come from and have taken the time to really reflect on what race means to you and your relationships.

Take a moment to reflect on your racial literacy and socialization experiences by responding to these questions:

Do you remember having conversations with your family about how to approach certain race-related situations or encounters? If so, what were they like?

_____

_____

While growing up, what did you learn about the historical and contemporary experiences of your racial group(s) from your family? School? Media?

_____

_____

_____

How does it make you feel when you reflect on the history and contemporary experiences of your racial group(s) in the United States?

_____

_____

_____

What (implicit or explicit) messages do you remember receiving from your family about how your racial group was supposed to act? What about other racial groups?

_____

_____

_____

_____

Take a minute to review your answers to the questions above. Did you get a sense of what your family and community taught you about the racial group or groups you are a member of? Were there any new insights you gained about how racism might manifest in your life? Or lessons you received that you now recognize as racial literacy skills?

We hope the questions provided you with a clearer picture of your racial identity, group(s), and socialization, and how they've guided you to navigate your relationships and social settings. For our White readers, you may have limited experience reflecting on your racial identity and socialization. We hope these questions increase your awareness of how race and racism have mattered in your life and in BIPOC communities as well, and that by developing racial literacy skills, you'll be able to practice antiracism.

For our BIPOC readers, we know from both the research and our lived experience that our communities have used racial identity, socialization, and literacy to build up our individual and community resources (such as the Black church tradition) so that we can maintain our health and spirits. If you feel that you did not develop racial literacy skills growing up, don't feel discouraged. You can always cultivate racial literacy as an adult. In a recent book, Howard Stevenson (2014), professor and clinical and consulting psychologist, describes one approach to developing racial literacy that involves learning to "read" a racially stressful situation, "recast" the situation through use of mindfulness strategies, and then ultimately "resolve" the encounter.

Of course, to successfully do this work, it's important for us to be on the same page about what racism actually is.

A CLOSER LOOK: RACISM

Racism is a system by which advantages and disadvantages are conferred based on our racial identities and where they fall within the racial hierarchy. And it is a system in which those higher on the racial hierarchy—White people, or the groups who are most White-adjacent—have been advantaged throughout our country's history by policies, laws, and practices that reinforce their power and privilege while restricting the resources and opportunities of those lower in the hierarchy (Wellman 2000; Williams, Lawrence, and Davis 2019).

Racism operates in many ways. It works on cultural levels, in the way that White American or Eurocentric cultures are held to be the norm from which all other non-European cultures diverge (Pieterse and Powell 2016). It works on an individual or personal level, in that you can experience racism in your interactions with other people based on your group memberships and how you've been socialized to behave in a racist society (Jones 2000). Racism also works on institutional or structural levels so that systems within society discriminate against BIPOC and limit the opportunities they have to find housing, jobs, reliable health care, and other important resources (Pieterse and Powell 2016).

And finally, racism can be internalized: by accepting, as a member of a racial group deemed "inferior" within the racial hierarchy, the messages we get about our abilities and our inherent worth as a human being. When one experiences racism on this internalized level, they may come to dislike and disdain those who look like them—and even themselves (Jones 2002).

Throughout the handbook, we will touch on each of these levels of racism, discussing what they look like and what you can do to change them, whether through yourself, your relationships, or your community. The particular strategies you use to cultivate antiracist practice will also depend on what kind of racism is being addressed. For instance, when we examine individual racism, it will matter whether you were the target, the perpetrator, or a bystander during the interactions in question. If you're a BIPOC reader, you may have to process more experiences of being a target or a bystander in a racist incident. If you're a White reader, you might grapple more often with being or knowing a perpetrator or a bystander—or with the experience of not having recognized racism or been willing to recognize it.

Meanwhile, with cultural and institutional racism, all groups are impacted: in positive ways for more advantaged racial groups and negative ways for less advantaged ones. White people, for instance, can often count on institutions to treat them fairly, as individuals, whereas BIPOC may confront being seen in stereotypical ways or denied certain opportunities.

A Note about Bias

Because we are all shaped by the ways race and racism play out in society, we all hold biases about racial groups at an unconscious level. That unconscious, or implicit, bias has been shown to have implications in areas ranging from education to criminal justice. For instance, studies have shown that implicit bias crops up in how preschool students are viewed by their teachers (Gilliam et al. 2016); it's also reflected in criminal justice decisions when people who were viewed as looking "more Black" (i.e., darker skin and more African features) were more likely to receive harsher sentences (Eberhardt 2019).

As you move through this handbook, you'll reflect on how unconscious bias may be playing out in interpersonal relationships or decisions, in professional settings, or even in your personal life. By increasing your awareness of unconscious bias, you may be able to shift negative behaviors and thought patterns.

WHAT'S NEXT?

In this chapter, we explored areas of understanding that form the foundation for antiracist work: what race is, how we're socialized to understand it and our racial identities, and how White supremacy creates a racial—and, ultimately, racist—hierarchy that restricts resources and respect for BIPOC.

We want you to take the information you've learned (or been reminded of) and any insight you've gained from the reflection exercises to take the next steps toward cultivating antiracist practice in your life. The subsequent chapters will help you address potential barriers. Taking an active stance against racist oppression may require a shift in your thinking. You will need to reflect on how you view yourself, others, and systems of oppression.

When you make the commitment to cultivate antiracist practice, you will see shifts in your behavior, relationships, and the ways you engage in your community—in turn changing yourself, your relationships, and your community for the better.

MINDFUL MOMENT: *Intersectionality*

We want to take a moment here to introduce the concept of intersectionality. The legal and critical race theory scholar Kimberlé Crenshaw (2016) describes intersectionality as the convergence of multiple forms of oppression based on the identities and social positions you hold. From an intersectional perspective, the experience of being a Black woman would be shaped by both racial and gender discrimination. A cisgender Black woman lesbian would also contend with the impact of heterosexism.

Take a moment to review various components of social identity. First, list how you identify, then think about whether advantages or disadvantages might come with your membership in each social group, and check the appropriate column.

	Advantage	Disadvantage
Race		
Ethnicity		
Gender		
Sexual Orientation		
Ability		
Religion		
Age		
Socioeconomic Status		
Immigration Status		
Language		

As you can see, we move through the world with a multifaceted social identity through which we may be advantaged and disadvantaged at the same time in various contexts. Our experiences at the intersection of identity and discrimination shape how we engage in the world and influence how we will cultivate antiracist practices in our lives.

CHAPTER 2

Educating Yourself—
Taking Responsibility

In this next chapter, we are going to build upon the reflection we encouraged in the previous chapter and focus on how to make the commitment to be antiracist—and how we can turn that commitment into action. You may be asking yourself "What can I do?" and "Where do I start?"

We'll emphasize three answers to these questions:

1. Raise your awareness of race and racism;

2. Increase your knowledge of race and racism to broaden your perspective; and

3. Think about your spheres of influence and take action.

Let's start with raising your awareness—a process you've already begun, which we'll dive deeper into now.

RAISE YOUR AWARENESS: FOSTER CRITICAL CONSCIOUSNESS

In the previous chapter, we explored what we mean when we talk about race and racism. We also took a deeper look at racial identity (what race means to you as an individual) and racial literacy (your ability to understand race and its role in inequality and oppression). A key aspect of raising awareness is developing a critical consciousness or "the capacity to critically reflect and act upon one's sociopolitical environment" (Diemer et al. 2006, 445). Brazilian educator and philosopher Paulo Freire originated the concept of *critical consciousness*, or *conscientization*, in his book *The Pedagogy of the Oppressed*. For Freire—and the many scholars across disciplines, including psychology, influenced by his seminal work—critical consciousness is a tool for raising awareness about how oppression shapes our environments, and how to challenge that oppression.

Critical consciousness is a way for you to start to cultivate antiracist practice. You may have noticed certain dynamics about race and racism before; fostering critical consciousness can help you see them in a new way.

Think back to the multiple levels of racism you read about in chapter 1. When you see how interpersonal or structural racism plays out in your life, or hear about it from someone else or on the news, you might ask yourself the questions suggested by liberation psychologist Lillian Comas-Díaz (2016, 260), which include: Who benefits from racism? Against whom is racism directed? To what end? As your critical consciousness grows, you'll find yourself asking these or similar questions about what you see in the world.

At the same time as your critical consciousness is expanding, your racial literacy will continue to develop as well. You should be better able to extend your racial literacy into what education professor Sonya Horsford (2014) refers to as *racial realism,* or the ability to acknowledge the history and significance of race and racism, rather than falling back into ignorance, indifference, or denial. Of course, this won't happen overnight. But as you become more consistent with critical reflection, your racial literacy skills will get stronger and you'll be better prepared to keep moving forward with your antiracism practice.

EXERCISE: Raising Your Critical Consciousness as a Daily Practice

To help you raise your awareness and foster critical consciousness, let's do a journal exercise. Over the next three days, take note of at least one thing each day that you have read or heard about race and/or racism: something you saw on the news, read about, or talked about with a friend or family member.

Day One

What happened and who was involved?

_____

_____

_____

In what ways did race and/or racism show up?

_____

_____

How did the dynamic(s) you noticed reinforce the racial hierarchy? What level of racism was at play?

_____

_____

How did you feel during the encounters you witnessed or experienced? How did you respond?

_____

_____

_____

Day Two

What happened and who was involved?

_____

_____

_____

In what ways did race and/or racism show up?

_____

_____

How did the dynamic(s) you noticed reinforce the racial hierarchy? What level of racism was at play?

_____

_____

How did you feel during the encounters you witnessed or experienced? How did you respond?

_____

_____

_____

Day Three

What happened and who was involved?

_____

_____

_____

In what ways did race and/or racism show up?

_____

_____

How did the dynamic(s) you noticed reinforce the racial hierarchy? What level of racism was at play?

_____

_____

How did you feel during the encounters you witnessed or experienced? How did you respond?

_____

_____

_____

At the end of the third day, review what you've written and notice the patterns, major themes, and feelings that emerged. Also reflect on the ways on how you likely noticed more about race and racism because you were tuned in. This intentional tuning in is *awareness-raising*

Through the process of raising your awareness and fostering a more critical consciousness, you may also have become aware of gaps in your knowledge about how race and racism were showing up in your life. As we touched on in previous chapters, people across racial groups have had limited exposure to the history of race and racism in the United States. Fortunately for us, we can always increase our knowledge, and next, we'll discuss a range of ways to do just that.

INCREASE YOUR KNOWLEDGE TO BROADEN YOUR PERSPECTIVE

Earlier in this workbook, we discussed the racial hierarchy in the United States: Whiteness valued at a premium, anti-Blackness sustained in policy and practice, and colonization and discrimination against Indigenous and other people of color leading to chronic threats to the health and well-being of BIPOC. We asked you to recognize the impact of race and racism on all of our lives and to reflect on the racial group(s) to which you belong. Some of you may have realized that although you want to be antiracist, there's a lot you don't know about race and racism—and that it's on you to learn more. Identifying resources to broaden your perspective about race and racism will help you on your way.

We know that educating ourselves about race and racism is not so simple. As we've discussed in this workbook, this engagement can be stressful at times. You may feel that you're too busy to really make the effort, or that it all seems too overwhelming. Maybe you believe it will be depressing, or you don't know where to look.

The good news is that there are a number of quality resources that can help increase your knowledge and lay a solid foundation for antiracist practice. Whether you prefer to read books or articles, such as Ijeoma Oluo's *So You Want to Talk about Race*, scroll through Twitter accounts or blogs like the *Psychology of Radical Healing* blog (https://www.psychologytoday.com/us/blog/healing-through-social-justice), refer to syllabi like the one curated by psychology professor Helen Neville and colleagues, view films, or enroll in classes or workshops, there is no shortage of good resources for you to explore.

For our BIPOC readers, your lived experience with racism and discrimination and the racial socialization you experienced growing up can be supplemented by resources about your community's experience with race and racism and about the experiences of other communities of color. Take this opportunity to broaden your perspective. Challenge yourself to question and work through any stereotypes that you may have accepted.

And for Indigenous people and other people of color who are not Black, make the effort to learn more about anti-Blackness and the extent to which it may have been internalized to some extent by other communities of color, including yours. Internalized racism and anti-Blackness are challenges to solidarity work, but they can be worked through to raise our awareness about our community's history and strengths.

We also want to stress that for White allies, it is important to take the initiative to educate yourself, and not expect your BIPOC friends, family, or colleagues to educate you. Yes, there will be times that you will need to listen to and receive necessary feedback from BIPOC—and to recognize that many BIPOC have been doing antiracist work for quite some time—but the responsibility to learn about your racial identity, how race has shaped White and BIPOC communities, and how we're all affected by racism as a system lies ultimately with you.

Although this responsibility lies with each of us, we don't have to do this work alone. We encourage you to find opportunities to engage with peers who are in similar places on the journey and draw on supportive interactions with them to help sustain your efforts. This support will shore up your courage and commitment.

Recognize Your Spheres of Influence

You might be thinking that now that you've put some time into raising your awareness, fostering critical consciousness, and increasing your knowledge, you're ready to jump into action. Or you might feel that you have so much more to learn before you can shift into action. We suggest feeling out what timing is best for you and recognizing how to balance learning with doing.

One way to maintain that balance is to recognize what psychologist Beverly Daniel Tatum (2007) has referred to as your *spheres of influence* or those places where you are most able to make an impact. Your spheres of influence might be with your family, at your place of work, where you worship, or in an online community. No matter where they might be, your spheres of influence are the spaces where you can take what you've been learning about race and racism, to put antiracist practice into action.

Tatum talks about the courage we all need to commit to making change in our spheres of influence, and this is important. It is not always easy to speak up about racism or to challenge stereotypes that our families and friends may hold. But we encourage you to keep your courage so that you can take action to put antiracism into practice.

Use the space below to list two or three of your spheres of influence: for instance, your family, school, neighborhood, or workplace. Then, jot down which people you engage with in each of these spheres, and how you might be able to work toward antiracism with them. Discuss what you find promising about the possibilities to make change as well as any fears you have about taking antiracist action in these areas.

_____

_____

_____

_____

_____

_____

_____

_____

In addition to courage, we also need humility for this work so that our egos don't get in the way of our authentic engagement. For those readers who have been advantaged by race or hold powerful positions in their spheres of influence, it is your responsibility to listen to the voices and experiences of those who have been marginalized by the racial hierarchy and the impact of racism—even when those who've been marginalized hold you accountable for your privilege in ways you may experience as uncomfortable or unfair. In the next chapter, we'll talk more about the dynamics around power and privilege, and why it's so important to confront power and privilege if we want to authentically engage in antiracist practice.

CHAPTER 3

What's Power (And Privilege) Got to Do With It?

In the previous chapter, we encouraged you to shift your perspective by educating yourself as a way of taking responsibility and confronting stereotypes. A key aspect of this education is becoming more aware of our country's living history of race and racism, which is ongoing and ever-present. This increased awareness will help you to better recognize the opportunities presented to you—to not only shift your mindset but to also actually move into antiracist action. At the core of race and the dynamics of racism are power and privilege.

This chapter will take a closer look at how power and privilege can complicate our efforts to be antiracist. Remember, just because these issues are complicated or challenging doesn't mean those efforts aren't needed—we must do our best to move forward despite the challenge. We can continue to dig deeper into what's making our efforts more challenging. Let's start with getting clearer about what we mean by power and privilege.

POWER IN THE RACIAL HIERARCHY

Earlier, we discussed the American racial hierarchy, wherein racial groups are organized according to how much society thinks they're "worth." In this hierarchy, Whiteness is most valued and Blackness is most devalued. The closer a given group is to Whiteness, the more advantage it's given; the further it gets from Whiteness, the more disadvantages it must confront. Accordingly, anti-Blackness plays a central role, along with White supremacy, in shaping how racism is experienced and expressed across racial groups. And racism and White supremacy don't just determine how valuable each racial group is thought to be; they determine how much power a given racial group will hold.

Power exists when a person or group holds an advantaged position and is able to access and control resources because of that power (Neal and Neal 2011). Being able to exert agency and influence is one component of power (Patel, Tabb, and Sue 2017). Similar to our understanding of racism as a system of advantages and disadvantages, based on race and expressed across multiple levels, the dynamics of power are systemic and multidimensional. As a result, we might hold—or lack—power at the individual, interpersonal, or interactional level (across the interactions we have with others), and at both intragroup and intergroup levels (within and between the groups we're part of). In other words, the power you hold and your ability to express it can vary, depending on the context (Pinderhughes 1989; 2017).

A helpful way to broaden your understanding about power dynamics is by thinking of the expression of power in the following ways: *power over, power to, power with,* and *power within* (Pinderhughes 2017). *Power over* occurs when individuals or groups exert influence or privilege over others. An example would include a judge handing down a ruling in a court case. *Power to* occurs when individuals or groups have the ability to make and enact decisions—for example, when you are able to marshal the resources needed to effect change in your life, i.e., move to a new home or change careers. *Power with* occurs when individuals or groups take collaborative and collective action. Current examples abound of multiracial and multigenerational groups of people coming together to protest injustices. Finally, *power within* exists when individuals develop their abilities/skills and foster self-confidence. This expression of power manifests when we have the time and energy to develop skills and feel confident expressing ourselves; for example, learning an instrument and performing in a recital, or practicing and delivering a speech or presentation.

REFLECTION EXERCISE: Power, Race, and Racism

Which expressions and experiences of power do you most relate to? Use the chart below to reflect on your experiences with power dynamics related to race and racism. Describe how you may have expressed or experienced power across dimensions and how you felt in those moments. Taking the time to reflect on how power has impacted your experiences with race and racism can help clarify how you can best prepare for taking antiracist action in the future both by taking responsibility for the power you hold and understanding the power held by the people you encounter and confront.

Power Dimension	Describe an experience you have had with this particular power dimension as it relates to race and racism.	What feelings arose for you during this experience?
Power Over		
Power To		
Power With		
Power Within		

Completing this activity will give you a snapshot of what it's like to negotiate these levels of power in day-to-day life. Your experiences with the "power over" dimension may highlight times when you felt vulnerable as others exerted influence over you. Or you may have felt guilty remembering when you held power over some other individual or group (or witnessed others holding this power). On the other hand, thinking about your experiences of the "power to" may remind you that there are spheres in which you do have the influence necessary to make changes when confronting racial discrimination or racially stressful encounters. Reflections on the "power with" dimension might illustrate the power of solidarity and the impact of working together with allies and others in your community to confront racism. Finally, your experiences in the "power within" dimension can help you recognize the strengths you already possess that you can use as you pursue antiracist action.

What about Privilege?

We want to take time here to talk a bit more about *privilege*—which is related to, but distinct from, power. While power is the ability to access and control resources and exert influence (with advantaged groups often holding more power than disadvantaged groups), privilege encompasses the unearned benefits that advantaged groups have by virtue of their status in hierarchical and oppressive systems (Case, Iuzzini, and Hopkins 2012). You may be familiar with the notion of White privilege described by Peggy McIntosh (1988) in her seminal piece, "White Privilege: Unpacking the Invisible Knapsack." In this piece, McIntosh likens White privilege to an invisible knapsack filled with unearned benefits that White people have access to (and are often unaware of), but BIPOC do not. An interesting counterpart to White privilege is what education professor Nolan Cabrera (2017) refers to as *White immunity,* or the protection White people generally receive from the disparate racial treatment and discriminatory racial encounters experienced by BIPOC communities (such as increased scrutiny from law enforcement or redlining, which are practices in real estate that restrict if and where Black families are able to buy homes).

What Would Fighting Power and Privilege Look Like for You?

Let's take time here and look back on a Mindful Moment exercise on intersectionality from chapter 1. We asked you to reflect on aspects of your identity where you are more or less advantaged—your points of power and privilege.

For BIPOC readers, power and privilege may exist in the aspects of your identity that give you an advantage, such as higher socioeconomic status or heterosexuality. We want you to increase your awareness of how you negotiate the power and privilege of your membership in these advantaged groups as you work with others to bring about antiracist change.

For people of color who are not Black or Indigenous, you likely hold some degree of racial power or privilege because of this; also, you may encounter anti-Black and/or anti-Indigenous racism expressed by friends and family, and you'll need to decide if and how you will respond. These conversations and interactions can be challenging because of the potential for conflict and challenging emotions such as fear of losing relationships, being misunderstood, and being the recipient of others' anger (discussed in chapter 8).

For our White readers, the power and privilege that accompany membership in the most advantaged group in our country's racial hierarchy are dynamics you must confront as you engage in antiracist practice. This means becoming conscious of the ways power and privilege may make your life easier than the lives of BIPOC around you, whether or not you've noticed or processed this much before. To continue an example from earlier in this chapter, consider how you are usually allowed to enjoy shopping in a store without being followed by salespeople or security.

There will also be times when your power and privilege themselves can be used as a platform to challenge racism that might be expressed in your presence. These inflection points are opportunities for you to move from being a bystander to being an ally who is an active agent of antiracism.

Reflections on Power and Privilege

Use the space below to think back on your experiences with race, racism, power, and privilege as a White person or someone who is BIPOC. Describe an instance when you recognized the power and privilege you held as a member of a more advantaged group—or a time when you recognized that you did not have the same level of power and privilege as others. This could be an interaction with family or friends, at work, or within your community. Reflect on how you negotiated that interaction: Who did you engage with? How did you feel? Did any tension arise? And if so, how did you work through it?

_____

_____

_____

_____

_____

Finally, knowing what you know now about power and privilege, what might you have done differently to be a more effective antiracist change agent?

_____

_____

_____

_____

_____

Being honest with ourselves about how power and privilege play out in our lives allows us to show up authentically in our efforts to bring about antiracist change. In the next part of the handbook, we'll look at some of the barriers that may arise as we work to be antiracist (and take a deeper dive into privilege) as well as how we can shift our perspectives and liberate our minds as we continue to grow into antiracist change agents.

PART 2

Addressing Barriers, Shifting Perspectives, and Liberating Our Minds

The chapters in Part 2 will guide you through the process of addressing psychological barriers to antiracism and embracing psychological and political liberation. As you continue on this journey, it's important to consider not only what you are against (racism) but also what you are committed to (justice and liberation).

You likely picked up this book because you want to actively resist racism in the larger society and within your personal life. But there are systems that actively work to maintain racism not only politically and economically but also psychologically. And there are barriers around and within each of us that we must overcome: avoidance, indifference, guilt, ignorance, ego, fear, and even unconsciously blaming people of color for the oppression they experience.

These chapters will help you identify and confront the ways in which the fatigue and trauma that racism has caused you may hinder your engagement in antiracism work. Each chapter will explain one barrier and raise your consciousness around how this barrier works in your life and the lives of others, and how you can overcome it. In addition to providing specific strategies for moving toward antiracism, the chapters will give you tools to shift into a mindset of liberation—to live your life in such a way that you continue to liberate your mind and the systems around you.

Before we begin this part, let us take a look at your awareness of the psychological barriers you are currently facing. The following is a list of barriers that we will address in the chapters of this workbook. Please rank them from most challenging for you personally (1) to least relevant to your journey (5). This may give you a sense of where in Part 2 you'd like to begin.

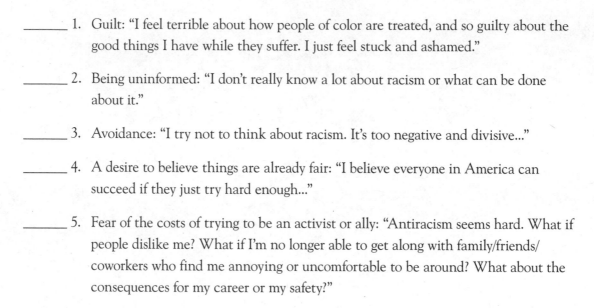

_____ 1. Guilt: "I feel terrible about how people of color are treated, and so guilty about the good things I have while they suffer. I just feel stuck and ashamed."

_____ 2. Being uninformed: "I don't really know a lot about racism or what can be done about it."

_____ 3. Avoidance: "I try not to think about racism. It's too negative and divisive…"

_____ 4. A desire to believe things are already fair: "I believe everyone in America can succeed if they just try hard enough…"

_____ 5. Fear of the costs of trying to be an activist or ally: "Antiracism seems hard. What if people dislike me? What if I'm no longer able to get along with family/friends/ coworkers who find me annoying or uncomfortable to be around? What about the consequences for my career or my safety?"

You may not know which barriers are the biggest for you, and that's fine—just take a guess. Then, at the end of this section, you can look back to see how accurate your predictions were.

Regardless of your ranking, we encourage you to complete all of the chapters in Part 2, even if not in the order they are here, because sometimes we have blind spots that get illuminated on the journey.

CHAPTER 4

"I Just Can't Think about It": Overcoming Avoidance

Avoidance is a behavior or action one takes to escape difficult feelings or thoughts. We may avoid people, places, conversations, or circumstances as a way of reducing anxiety or discomfort. And, when it comes to racism in our society, many of us avoid the feelings and thoughts it can bring up.

There's a common assumption that people are choosing to be either consciously racist or antiracist, but the reality is: many people haven't really made a choice at all. They may not consider themselves "political" or they may be conflict-avoidant. They may also benefit from the current system, and not want to give that up. But the result is that injustices go unaddressed: some of us face real harm, and others end up profiting from the ways others are oppressed.

To overcome avoidance, we must acknowledge it and begin to consider its roots. As James Baldwin wrote in a 1962 essay for the *New York Times* entitled "As Much Truth as One Can Bear": "Not everything that is faced can be changed, but nothing can be changed until it is faced." In this chapter, we will provide strategies to overcome the ways you might avoid racism—in the ways you think, the ways you feel, and the actions you take as a person in the world—so that you can adopt an antiracism mindset and live an antiracist lifestyle.

DO YOU AVOID RACISM?

The following statements are examples of ways we often practice avoiding racism in what we choose to recognize and respond to in any racism we might encounter. To better understand the ways you might be avoiding, please score each of these statements using the following scale:

A. Strongly Agree   B. Agree   C. Disagree   D. Strongly Disagree

_____ 1.   I don't like to follow the news. It's too negative.

_____ 2.   If it's not positive, I don't want to hear about it.

_____ 3.   When people make racist comments, I prefer to ignore them.

_____ 4.   My spiritual practice is to detach from the negative and only focus on gratitude.

_____ 5.   I try to avoid conversations about racism because people get angry.

_____ 6.   I try not to make comments or post anything that could be interpreted as political because the conflict and drama are just not worth it.

_____ 7.   I think if people could stop focusing so much energy on racism, things would probably get better.

If you agreed to any of the statements above, this indicates some level of avoidance around anti-racism work. There are any number of reasons we avoid responding to racism in day-to-day life and we may be conditioned to act in racist ways. For instance, your avoidance may be rooted in anxiety. You may have anxiety about encountering the distress of others or feeling distressed yourself. Some of us grew up in cultures, religions, and/or families that taught us that all "negative emotions" were unacceptable and should be avoided at all costs. So, if we are taught that anger, sadness, distress, fear, outrage, or even suffering itself are intolerable, we will avoid potential triggers of those emotions.

Also, many of us, especially in Western societies, may have grown up with norms and decorum that made it "impolite" to talk about race and racism, leaving us unprepared for how uncomfortable honest conversations about racism often are—and how vital it is to have them. When we avoid confronting racism when it emerges in our lives, we allow it to flourish. Unchecked racism persists and multiplies.

To be antiracist in attitude and action requires intentionally tuning into the reality of racism, instead of mindlessly or purposefully checking out. And it requires doing this even when the work of confronting racism—speaking up when someone says something racist, sitting with and advocating for someone who's being racially harassed to protect them or show them support, filming an incident in which law enforcement is violating someone's rights, or attending a march or a protest—is tough, potentially dangerous, or painful. While later in the book we will discuss the necessity of taking time and space for restoration and rest, the general stance of antiracism is engagement, not avoidance.

To confront racism—both psychologically, in examining your ways of thinking, and behaviorally, by acting in ways that confront and interrupt acts of racism—requires the ability to tolerate some level of distress. Again, for some of us, a low capacity to tolerate distress may come from having grown up in a very protective environment in which we were conditioned to believe we were not capable, effective, or resilient enough to navigate the world in general or racism in particular, so we have to keep our heads down and not make waves. A low capacity to tolerate distress may also be rooted in trauma we experienced in the past, moments in which we were flooded with overwhelming, dangerous feelings, in events or circumstances that had the potential to cause us harm—for instance, if we experienced intense racism, especially growing up, or some other form of abuse.

In an attempt to prevent this emotional flooding from happening again, we may consciously or unconsciously condition ourselves to avoid all potential triggers or reminders of being unsafe. This may lead us to believe that others need to do the heavy lifting for us—we're just not strong enough to handle confrontation or deal with the consequences of speaking up when we see racism happening—or even that no one should do it because it's too hard.

The key to changing these patterns of avoidance is to understand *why* you avoid—to understand your privilege and oppression within the racial hierarchy, and how your past experiences have influenced the way you behave today—and from there, to build your capacity to tolerate the distress that antiracism can cause.

Distress tolerance is a skill emphasized in dialectical behavioral therapy (DBT)—the ability to find ways to calm yourself and regulate negative emotions during difficult moments. When our distress tolerance is low, we often become emotionally dysregulated in the moments we experience racism: tearful, overwhelmed, or angry. All of which is understandable because racism is deeply personal. When we encounter it or witness it, we're inevitably encountering and witnessing the devaluation and dehumanization of other people. And it's only natural that this will cause us pain, humiliation, anger, and more emotions that we'd prefer to avoid.

But here, another idea from DBT is useful: dialectical thinking. *Dialectical thinking* is the ability to perceive issues from multiple vantage points and then arrive at a psychological state that allows you to live with and reconcile the various contradictions. The reality is that racism is a big system, and it's been around a long time. So it's only natural to feel powerless, overwhelmed, and even hopeless to change it.

At the same time, it's true that we have agency, capacity, and clarity—often, more than we know. You're exercising them right now, by reading this book and committing to antiracist practice in your life, and you can continue to by doing all you can to combat racism in your life and others'. First, it's helpful to work to change patterns of avoiding racism to patterns of confronting racism, and to learn to tolerate the feelings that this can bring up.

So, that's what we'll do in the rest of this chapter, starting with a look at the privileges each of us hold, and how those can lead us to avoid racism as both White people and BIPOC.

UNPACKING PRIVILEGE: GETTING PAST AVOIDANCE

Privilege is unearned benefit and authority to engage in attitudes, beliefs, and behaviors that perpetuate the status quo of racial and social inequity (Liu 2017). To have privilege does not mean you have not worked for anything in your life, but it does mean you are not penalized or blocked by the same barriers that face members of targeted or marginalized groups. For instance, if you're a White person, your race ensures that you are more likely to be seen favorably on a home loan, in a job application, on a dating app, and in a medical facility—but a BIPOC person is more likely to face racist assumptions that they are less qualified for a home loan or job they want, less desirable or attractive, or less deserving of quality health care. Sometimes, when it comes to taking part in a protest for their rights, they can even be seen as un-American. The ability to be seen as more intelligent, beautiful, or moral as a result of being White—as opposed to being stigmatized based on racial stereotypes—is a clear form of privilege.

There are different forms of privilege: White privilege, male privilege (by which those of us who are or present as male receive more respect and consideration than those who do not), heterosexual privilege (by which privilege is given to those who are heterosexual and straight over those who are not), and ability privilege (by which those who are "able" are privileged over those who are differently abled), among others.

In terms of racism, White people benefit from White privilege because systems reward them for their Whiteness while penalizing BIPOC for their racial identities. This includes documented White privilege in the education system, criminal (in)justice system, medical system, media, banking, and even the mental health system, among others (Liu, Pickett, and Ivey 2007; Pepin 2016; Pewewardy and Severson 2003; Torino 2015). More specifically, White children are more likely to be presented with members of their race as examples of great writers, artists, scientists, and contributors to society-at-large (Office of the Surgeon General 2001). This is not because BIPOC have not contributed to the world in every discipline but because racism is rampant within curriculum development. In the courts, studies reveal that potential jurors are more likely to believe a Black or Brown person is guilty of a crime than a White person, even when the evidence is the same (Zach 2015). If you are White, you are far less likely to be killed by police, even if you are armed and have killed someone. If you are White, you do not have to prepare your children for encounters with people who want to harm them because of their race. In the media, White actors are more likely to have a range of character opportunities to portray, while BIPOC are often invisible or in stereotypical roles such as service professionals or criminals (Isaacs 2011). Racism exists in banking, with identical loan applications being treated more favorably if the applicant identifies as White than as Black. And it exists in the health care system, with White people being more likely to have mental health insurance, to be free from the stress of racism, and to have access to treatment provided by someone of their own race, utilizing interventions developed with them in mind (McGuire and Miranda 2008). Across fields and social settings, having cultural names that are associated with being non-White can be a barrier to opportunities regardless of your qualifications (Pew Research Center 2019). It is also a form of White privilege to not have to think about, acknowledge, or combat racism, while continuing to benefit from a system that favors White people (Pew Research Center 2019).

When you occupy a privileged enough position in society that you are not a target of racism—and in fact, you benefit from racism, passively or even actively—then avoiding racism you witness or participate in becomes an act of agreement and cooperation with racism. If you choose to opt out of antiracism work to avoid discomfort, you are deciding that *I am unwilling to be inconvenienced or uncomfortable in order to participate in creating a more just society.* It is important that you care enough about equity that you continue on this journey of antiracism instead of retreating to avoidance.

In that spirit, if you're a White reader, take a second to think about the privilege you have, as a White person, and based on any other markers of your status that intersect with your Whiteness: your wealth, level of education, gender, and so on.

Have there been times in your life when your privilege became apparent to you? Did you respond? How do you think these moments affected the BIPOC around you?

_____

_____

_____

If you're a BIPOC reader, think about specific instances of White privilege—and White avoidance—that you've witnessed. What was it like to experience this?

_____

_____

_____

Finally, if you've never noticed White privilege much before, whether you're BIPOC or White, just reflect on the thoughts and feelings that came up as you read this section.

_____

_____

Of course, privilege is not limited to White people. Among BIPOC, there is benefit given to people of color who are not targeted by anti-Black racism—the specific forms of discrimination and prejudice against Black people, who have inherited a unique legacy of enslavement and segregation in America—as well as those who've been given light-skin privilege, which deems lighter-complexioned people more safe, intelligent, attractive, and valuable than their darker-complexioned counterparts. Light-skin privilege is given based on colorism, which is a manifestation of the false ideology of White superiority. *Colorism* is the valuing of people of color who are of a lighter skin complexion over those who are darker, and it has roots in colonialism and enslavement. Colorism has persisted across generations and exists across racial/ethnic groups. As a result of the favoritism and preferential treatment lighter-complexioned BIPOC receive from White people and institutions, some BIPOC have experienced rejection or distrust from darker-complexioned BIPOC.

Ultimately, though, the burdens of racism fall harder on BIPOC with darker complexions. And so, if you're a non-Black person or a BIPOC who has light-skin privilege, to avoid addressing racism is to continue to reap benefits from a system that advantages you to the detriment of Black people and other people of darker complexions. The same goes for those of us in BIPOC groups who have privilege based on our social class, education level, or affluence, and what kinds of regions and neighborhoods we can afford to live in. All of these are factors that can influence how others perceive us and how easy it is for us to navigate the world.

And if you're a BIPOC who benefits from privilege in some way, it falls to you to confront that if you want to be antiracist—meaning, to understand the privileges you hold, observe how they can affect your thinking and your behavior, change these patterns, and speak up for other BIPOC when you see them being oppressed. It is also important to acknowledge that those factors do not completely protect you from racism. The academic degrees you hold do not erase the negative assumptions that many people hold when they see you. It is, however, crucial that those BIPOC who benefit from racism, the falsehood of White superiority, and certain physical characteristics or socioeconomic positions that are deemed closer to the White ideal take an active stance in shifting from avoidance to engagement in antiracism.

If you're a BIPOC, take a moment to reflect on the racial privilege you have personally witnessed in BIPOC circles. Reflect on the ways you might have even benefited from the privileges you hold in BIPOC circles and in social or professional circles. Have you experienced non-Black BIPOC privilege and/or light skin privilege? Or as a BIPOC, have you experienced privilege related to educational level, religious affiliation, or sexuality that other BIPOC do not experience? If so, how does it affect you?

_____

_____

_____

If you have never noticed White privilege or non-Black BIPOC privilege before, please reflect on the thoughts and feelings that came up as you read this section.

_____

_____

_____

Again, because privilege is assigned to us, rather than something we ourselves create or claim, we often benefit from it while avoiding any confrontation around the ways we benefit. If you can become aware of the privileges that you and others have, you're more likely to be able to be an ally in situations where privilege is a factor.

Here are some ways you can resist White privilege and non-Black POC privilege when you see it:

1. When you are in a store and a worker skips a Black, Indigenous, or other person of color to serve you, step back and indicate that the BIPOC was there first.

2. When you are in a social setting and people are discussing BIPOC, or Black people in particular, in stereotypical ways, speak up and state that the statement made reflects a stereotype and does not apply to every member of that race.

3. Self-reflect on the areas in which you hold privilege and educate yourself about the experiences of those who are marginalized in ways that you are not. As you learn, pass on the knowledge to your friends and family.

4. At your job, speak up to advocate for a racially diverse pool of applicants, hires, and promotions to positions of power and initiatives.

5. Refuse to take credit or be given credit for the labor of Black, Indigenous, or other people of color, which is often attributed to White people in professional and social settings. Acknowledge the labor of BIPOC, which is often unappreciated.

Now that you've had a chance to consider your privilege, let's look at how you can overcome your avoidance around challenging your own privilege or the racism of others, whether you're White or BIPOC.

Overcoming Avoidance as a White Person

White people who avoid acknowledging racism believe they can thereby relieve themselves from the responsibility of working for racial justice. If you convince yourself or are convinced by others that calling out racism is unpatriotic, divisive, or results in White people being the targets of racism, then you don't have to feel uncomfortable with your disengagement and inactivity in the antiracism movement. Additionally, researchers found that White people are more comfortable participating in discussions about racism when the discussions are structured; in other words, when there is a guide or facilitator who controls the content of the conversation (Tittler and Wade 2019). The presence of a facilitator provides some relief from the fear that discussions of racism will result in extreme anger, rage, verbal attacks, or aggression. This fear is based on the racist stereotype that people of color are violent and threatening as well as the dehumanizing racist belief that people of color don't have full emotional lives. In both of these cases, avoiding acknowledging or addressing racism alleviates a sense of personal responsibility and fear of emotionally charged communication. While this may feel like a good solution temporarily, racism persists and will continue to reveal itself, cracking through the wall of denial.

Psychologist and professor Derald Wing Sue, a leading scholar on racism, recommends the following for facilitators of dialogues on racism: include acknowledging one's own racial biases; controlling the process, but not the content of the dialogue; giving verbal validation to those who make themselves vulnerable; and teaching others to be open to racial blunders they might make and criticism they might receive (2013). These facilitated conversations may happen occasionally in schools or corporations, but in everyday life, they are rare.

If you are a White person, name three things that have kept you from either acknowledging or addressing racism.

1. _____

2. _____

3. _____

What have you gained through your avoidance?

_____

_____

_____

_____

What has avoidance cost you? For example, are there certain relationships you've had that failed to flourish or ended as a result of your silence or denial of racism? Has harm come to BIPOC as a result of your disengagement?

_____

_____

_____

_____

Overcoming Avoidance as a BIPOC

For BIPOC, avoidance may be a coping strategy to deal with the potentially traumatizing impact of racism. You might try not to think about racism you've heard about or experienced in order to decrease distress, depression, and anxiety. While avoidance may alleviate distress temporarily, since it does not address racism, the oppressive systems persist and you are continuously subjected to additional violations and/or invalidations.

If you are a BIPOC, describe one time in the past year when you witnessed racism in person or through the media and managed your distress by trying not to think about it or talk about it.

_____

_____

_____

What did you gain by avoiding the thoughts or exchanges?

_____

_____

_____

While it is healthy at times to step away from the trauma of racism, if you always choose avoidance, what does your denial or silence cost you or others?

_____

_____

_____

_____

_____

MINDFULNESS: THE GIFT OF PRESENCE

One option, when it comes to shifting your behavior from compliance with racism to being actively antiracist, is to reframe your thoughts—to shift your perspective about an issue. For example, if you have the thought _It's easier not to think about racism_, it's important to shift that thought to something like _Racism exists, and we all have to think about and deal with it_, because racism depends on our active or tacit participation in it to continue, and it isn't something you can deny. However, it's also true that sometimes, instead of an absolute shift that requires an either/or dichotomy, it can be useful to broaden the frame to acknowledge that multiple frames can coexist. Here, again, thinking dialectically is useful. The narrow frame of avoidance may be thinking that racism can be hard, draining, and depressing, while at the same time, choosing to be present and engaged in efforts to combat racism can be inspiring, rewarding, and empowering. In other words, instead of giving into the temptation to opt out, let us consider that being present can be a gift.

Mindfulness is choosing to be present to the present moment with compassion and awareness. While mindfulness as a therapeutic practice combining Buddhist teachings and scientific studies was developed by Jon Kabat-Zinn, its roots are in Asian culture and predate the Western fascination with the approach. Similar constructs and practices are also observed in Native American medicine and ancient Egyptian (Kemetic) philosophy. Those who were not consumed in production and consumption knew and taught the gift of presence, stillness, and sacred silence, not as a strategy but as a way of life. You can adopt that philosophy as well in your journey into antiracism and liberation. You can choose not to stay stuck in the missed opportunities of the past or the fears of what racists will do in the future. Both of these can cause you to shut down and disengage. And you can choose to deal with the tough feelings that will inevitably arise when you do engage in antiracist work, rather than letting those tough feelings overwhelm you and steer you back toward passivity and inaction. Instead of getting stuck in thoughts of the past, fears of the future, or the pain that working for change will inevitably bring, tune in to the gift, the opportunity of this present moment, when you can show up for yourself and others to help shift the tide from racism to antiracism.

EXERCISE: Mindfully Thinking About Racism

Consider each of the following prompts. For each one, write what comes to mind as honestly and openly as you can. After you complete each sentence, take a cleansing full, slow breath.

1.   When I think about racism in my community, I feel emotions like:

   _____

2.   When I think about racism in the present, the images that come to mind are:

   _____

3.   When I think about racism in the present, in my body I feel:

   _____

4.   When I think about being a part of the movement toward racial justice—speaking out when I encounter racism in my life, supporting myself and others in doing antiracist work, and joining racial justice movements in my area—I feel emotions like:

   _____

5.   When I think about being a part of the movement toward racial justice, the image(s) that come to mind are:

   _____

6.   When I think about being a part of the movement toward racial justice, in my body I feel:

   _____

Racism Distress Tolerance Activities

In this part, we'll explore different practices you can use to increase your capacity to tolerate distress and help yourself heal when you're stressed and in pain: embodied healing, relaxation, emotional expression, expressive arts, sensation focus, socializing, and improving your environment. If you practice these strategies consistently in the abstract, and build yourself a routine of self-care and restoration, it'll be easier to summon skills like relaxation or sensation focus during a tense racist encounter or while trying to engage in antiracist action on behalf of a community member, and you'll learn to resist the temptation to engage in avoidance when these moments arise.

It's important to keep in mind that you're not simply learning how to cope with racism or tolerate racism; you're developing the capacity to manage the distress associated with racism so you can do the work of combating it. Avoidance leads to us adjusting to racism instead of challenging it—and Reverend Dr. Martin Luther King, Jr. warned against people adjusting to the dysfunction of racial oppression in this way (https://www.apa.org/monitor/features/king-challenge).

> So, these strategies are not aimed at increasing our ability to tolerate racism and racist acts and people but instead to give us the inner fortitude to dismantle, interrupt, and combat racism while we work for justice and liberation.

SOMATIC/EMBODIED HEALING

Somatic healing is body-oriented healing. Resmaa Menakem (2017), a body-centered psychotherapist and author who specializes in healing racialized trauma in our hearts and bodies, recommends that, in addressing racism, we begin by becoming more aware of our bodies. Embodied healing involves understanding the stress you're holding in your body and ways of releasing it. The next time you hear about or think about racism, try engaging in one of the following activities as you make room for the thoughts and feelings that arise. The movement options listed below are not a distraction, but rather, create the space in your mind and body to become aware of the tension that you're holding without drowning in it or stuffing it.

- Go for a walk
- Dance
- Do yoga
- Stretch your body

- Exercise
- Go for a bike ride
- Do martial arts
- Garden

RELAXATION

The next time you hear about, think about, or witness racism in a vicarious way (e.g., see a video clip online), try engaging in one of the following relaxation activities afterward. Again, the suggestion is not to distance yourself from your feelings but to give yourself permission to feel your feelings while taking care of yourself.

- Listen to a guided meditation or relaxing music

- Get a massage or give yourself a face, head, or neck massage

- Lie down or take a nap

- Take a few cleansing breaths

- Go for a drive

- Rock in a rocking chair

- Hug yourself

- Sit in the dark or in the sun

- Visualize the world as it would look with racial justice and equity

EMOTIONAL EXPRESSION

The next time you hear about, think about, or vicariously witness racism, try engaging in one of the following activities to express your feelings.

- Cry

- Journal

- Stomp or shout

- Squeeze a rubber ball

- Name your feelings and needs

- Visualize a drain as you feel the fullness of your feelings and then allow it to be released

- Think loving thoughts toward yourself and whoever was targeted

- Use the empty-chair technique, to role-play saying everything you would like to say to those who are engaging in the racist behavior

EXPRESSIVE ARTS

The next time you hear about, think about, or vicariously witness racism, try engaging in one of the following strategies, with a focus on making a vision of the antiracism future you're hoping and working to create.

- Create a collage

- Paint

- Sing or hum

- Write a poem and read it aloud

- Choreograph a dance

- Play an instrument

SENSATION FOCUS

The next time you hear about, think about, or vicariously witness racism, try engaging in one of the following strategies while you allow your feelings, thoughts, and needs to be present.

- Drink hot tea

- Light a scented candle or burn incense

- Eat something you enjoy

- Listen to nature sounds

- Hold an ice cube until it melts

- Place a cold washcloth on your face

- Put on lotion

- Put on scented oils or perfume

- Take a warm bath or shower

- Look out the window or take pictures

Socializing and Improving the Environment

Allison is a thirty-five-year-old White woman who works in a diverse setting. She is friendly to everyone, but does not have close friendships with any BIPOC. After seeing several news stories and social media posts about racism and police brutality, she reached out to a Black associate and left a tearful voice message about how terrible racism is.

The associate did not call her back because she did not have the energy or interest in comforting Allison or in being vulnerable about her pain with someone she doesn't consider a real friend. During a work Zoom call, Allison shared her distress about the news stories and called on the two coworkers of color by name to explain what police brutality was and how they felt about it. One coworker turned off her camera and the other coworker briefly described the latest police killing of a Black man and told the coworkers they could find more information through Google. The POC coworkers felt startled by Allison's demand, drained, and resentful about being put on the spot to share their pain at work.

Allison has had trouble sleeping since she saw the viral video of a Black man being killed on the street, with no one helping him. She wants others in her company to feel how she feels and to understand the seriousness of what's going on. She also feels confused and rejected by the three people of color she reached out to. She feels the only thing she can do is try to push the terrible videos out of her mind.

What's gone wrong in Allison's attempt to act on the pain she feels at the racist violence she's witnessed? While her feelings of unrest are understandable, and she's resisting the instinct to avoid racism altogether that traps so many of us—especially when we're privileged—she's responding to it in the worst possible way: by calling on coworkers of color to speak and to be representatives of their race, shouldering the burden of educating others about it, without regard for whether they want to be involved in what she's doing or whether it's even clear what she wants to do. It sends the message that her pain is the most important thing in the situation—that *it* needs assuaging, and she doesn't even notice the additional pain she's causing her coworkers in the process.

The next time you hear about, think about, or vicariously witness racism, try engaging in one of the following ways to connect with others and stand in solidarity with those who are also on the journey of antiracism and liberation—keeping your privilege and what you're asking of others in mind.

- Ask for support (within reason: if you're White, be mindful of not expecting BIPOC to be your emotional caretakers; they are dealing with stress and trauma of being the targets of racism, and your education is not their responsibility)

- Be with people who have a heart for antiracism

- Go to a religious or spiritual gathering that is affirming or nourishing

- Participate in collective meditation and/or prayer for racial justice

- Go to a social justice event—a community gathering committed to racial justice

- Listen to recordings or read the work of a racial justice activist you admire

- Research an organization that is doing the work of racial justice and explore if there are ways that you can volunteer and/or donate to support the work

Take a look at the activities above and select three activities that have been helpful to you in general or relating to racism in particular. These will be foundational for your distress plan as you move toward antiracism in your mindset and life.

1. _____

2. _____

3. _____

It's important that we also stretch ourselves or increase our toolbox. With that in mind, list three activities from the above list that you've never tried, either in general or related to racism, but that you're willing to try, to continue building your capacity to deal with the pain and discomfort antiracist work can bring.

1. _____

2. _____

3. _____

Before we move on, it's worth addressing another form of avoidance that often emerges in response to racism, particularly for those who are spiritual or religious—spiritual bypassing.

Spiritual Bypassing

Some of us justify avoidance of acknowledging and addressing racism by utilizing the psychological strategy of *spiritual bypassing*, which is the practice of using spiritual beliefs or practices as an excuse not to acknowledge psychological difficulties or problems (Welwood 2000). You might have heard about concepts like "toxic positivity," "toxic spirituality," and "toxic gratitude," which refer to a commitment to only focusing on positive emotions, denying any suffering or pain. People engaging in spiritual bypassing when confronted with racial injustice may respond with actions that imply (1) everyone needs to just forgive and move forward; (2) if we all detached and emptied ourselves of resentment, everyone would have more peace; or (3) whoever's upset needs to remember that someone else has it worse than them, so they should be grateful for whatever resolution they get. These kinds of messages are far from an antiracist mindset. They may well be intended to encourage others, and they may reflect a genuine desire that everyone involved in the situation be reconciled, but the impact is that people who experience racism are likely to feel unsupported, unheard, and unseen by these responses. When presented with racism, you want to choose to give your friend or coworker compassion—not denial. Choosing compassion and believing what they tell you as true lays the groundwork for challenging and disrupting racism, instead of permitting it to persist.

EXERCISE: Confronting Spiritual Bypassing

To confront spiritual bypassing, it is important for those who follow a particular spiritual or religious teaching to consider the ways their beliefs can be called upon to engage with and address suffering and oppression. Consider one fundamental teaching, value, or construct from your spiritual or religious belief system: for example, love, justice, community, or generosity. In the space below, write about how that spiritual teaching or value could relate to the call for antiracism and liberation itself.

_____

_____

_____

_____

_____

Mindful Movement

The closing activity for this chapter is mindful movement. (If walking is not accessible for you, please consider utilizing your wheelchair, other assisted device, or support person to move through space, or visualize yourself moving through space.) Mindful movement is moving through space at a slow pace, not rushing to where you want to go but observing yourself and your surroundings where you are.

For this exercise, as you walk outside or around your home, visualize yourself walking to embrace an antiracism mindset and life. Instead of running away from racism in an attempt to avoid it, picture yourself not alone but with people all over the world who are also committed to walking with compassion and courage toward justice. Instead of focusing on how and what you want to be at the end of this journey, make peace with where you are. You have begun to shift inwardly and perhaps even outwardly. Walk slowly, being aware of your breath and who you are right now, as you hold your values in your heart, mind, body, and spirit. Feel yourself present for the inner and outer work. Feel yourself present and capable of choosing to bear witness to the very real need for this work. Feel yourself breathing and moving forward.

CHAPTER 5

Freeing Our Minds from Being Stuck in Guilt

Lisa is a thirty-four-year-old Chinese American bisexual, spiritual but not religious woman who grew up in a wealthy, highly educated family. In college, she took classes on race and gender that confirmed her experiences of being treated as the model minority. She felt guilty for the times she observed Whites mistreating Black, Latinx, and Indigenous classmates and friends while praising her. She also felt guilt about the anti-Black racism that she heard from her parents and the pervasive colorism that resulted in her being treated better by her family than her darker-complexioned sisters. Additionally, Lisa feels guilty about the wealth and opportunities that she has had access to while she knows many other Chinese Americans, as well as other people of color, are struggling to survive. Lisa's guilt has resulted in her spending less time with her family and trying to hide her wealth from her friends, for fear of being judged or rejected for her privilege. She also often dresses in fashion trends set by Black people, in an attempt to show solidarity and connection.

Michelle is a twenty-six-year-old straight, middle-income, Christian White woman who grew up in a predominantly White area and attended a predominantly White school. She was taught by her parents, teachers, and church that everyone should be treated with respect and kindness. She was also taught that if she and others applied themselves, they would have good lives with financial security and the respect of the community. In alignment with that, she always worked hard in school and on her job, and she was frustrated by Black people; who she deemed to be "lazy" and "irresponsible," as evidenced by their unemployment rates, incarceration rates, and living conditions. When Michelle moved to a more diverse city and began listening to the experiences and history of BIPOC—how hard it often was for them to secure the resources she had always had and taken for granted, like good places to live, access to opportunities, and the right to be treated fairly by those around them—she was horrified. She felt terribly embarrassed and guilty for how much she didn't know and for the negative stereotypes she held about Black and Brown people. She also felt guilty about being part of a race that had done such harm to people of color. Michelle's extreme guilt left her silent or tearful and apologetic when BIPOC brought up issues of racism on the job and voiced frustration with the lack of action or support from White coworkers.

While the manifestation and experience of it are different, BIPOC and White people can both become immobilized by racism-related guilt. When we experience excessive guilt, we can become silent and disengaged even in the face of racism. And ultimately, that is a form of complicity: a way of siding with people who perpetrate racism. As Judith Herman notes in her book *Trauma and Recovery*, it is easy to side with perpetrators; all they require is our silence. And when we feel overwhelmed by guilt, we also often feel incapable of using our voice and our agency, which are two critical components of antiracism. On the other hand, excessive guilt can also cause us to idealize BIPOC or suffering itself in ways that are dehumanizing and harmful.

In this chapter, we will first explore the psychology of guilt, its consequences, and its potential benefits. Then we can look more specifically at the experience of guilt for BIPOC and then for White people. Finally, we'll provide you with some strategies of mindfulness and embodiment so you can begin to free yourself from guilt's immobilizing weight and move from being stuck in feeling bad to taking antiracist action and improving the world around you.

WHAT IS GUILT?

When it comes to racism, *guilt* is an emotional response that occurs when we receive benefits we know we have not earned—as with White privilege or certain kinds of privilege within BIPOC groups—or in moments when we're not acting in alignment with our values. You may experience racism-related guilt as a result of the times you didn't take action to address racism, or when you colluded with racism by your thoughts, words, or actions, the collective behavior of those of your race, and/or your passive receipt of benefits that are denied to others based on their race.

While your guilt can lead to getting stuck in fear, another possibility is to allow the guilt that comes from awareness to be a motivating factor that leads you to engage in working toward racial justice. To be antiracist, we must value racial justice and allow that value to guide our internal and external lives. So, continuing on your antiracist journey, your task in this chapter will be to explore the nature of the guilt you may feel, and to turn that guilt into fuel to practice everyday resistance to racism.

Exploring Your Guilt

Underneath the guilt, you feel may be a sense of grief: a sense of loss of the type of person you thought you were; who you thought your family members, loved ones, or friends were; and what you thought your nation was. Perhaps you believed that you were a good person with a good heart who would not stand by when injustice was occurring, only to find that somehow that's exactly what's happened. Or maybe you believed only monsters would be racists, and yet you find you're forced to acknowledge racism within yourself or from those you care about or from systems and institutions that you thought would be fair. You may also experience grief in the recognition that you've not fully lived up to who you want to be as it relates to the fight against racism. This grief merged with guilt can be a heavy weight, emotionally and even physically.

When we feel guilty, we need to consider our response to the guilty feeling: We can deny that we feel it at all; become stuck in it, constantly ruminating on how we feel, and never letting it go; or we can allow it to inspire corrective action. Consider how much a sense of guilt has been beyond your awareness or the ways in which it has been a heavy weight, keeping you overwhelmed and immobilized. Now consider what it would mean to transform the guilt into responsive, caring action.

EXERCISE: The Value of Justice

To reflect on justice as a value, select one of the songs below that is focused on justice and find a recording of it online. As you listen to it, as a beginning step toward embodiment, become aware of any reaction you may experience in your body. There is no one right response. Notice if the song calms you or energizes you. Do you find yourself swaying, clapping, sitting up in your chair, or leaning back? Where do you feel the song in your body? Allow yourself, including your physical body, to fully experience the sound.

"Sojourner's Battle Hymn," Sweet Honey in the Rock

"Redemption Song," Bob Marley

"A Change Is Gonna Come," Sam Cooke

"Formation," Beyoncé

"Fight the Power," Public Enemy

"Alright," Kendrick Lamar

"Miedo," Mala

"Mutiny," Mike "Witko" Cliff

"Bayan Ko," Freddie Aguilar

Write below your reflection about the sensations, emotions, images, and body awareness that came as you listened to the song that you selected:

_____

_____

_____

_____

_____

Why did we have you do this exercise? Listening to music is a form of *expressive arts therapy*, which is the intentional use of the arts to help you connect with your feelings and thoughts, express yourself, release distress, and integrate different aspects of yourself that might currently be at odds. This exercise is important because it causes you to be present with your awareness about injustice while the music helps to soothe you. When we are calmed yet engaged, we are mindful that we are not stuck. As you heard the song you selected, you were reminded that you're not in this fight for racial justice alone. The vocal artists and people all over the world are shifting or have shifted from guilt to engagement. As you read this chapter, try to remember to connect with yourself, emotionally, physically, mentally, and spiritually. Also remember that you're not alone in this journey.

BIPOC and Guilt

As you think about not being alone on this journey, we invite you to reflect on your experience as a BIPOC in relationship to other BIPOC community members of your race and of other races. When you're part of a group that experiences a traumatic event, including the trauma of oppression, you may experience survivor's guilt if you believe you've had a relatively good life in comparison to other members of your group. We see this experience in veterans and even survivors of childhood abuse who grew up in households where they received favorable treatment as compared to their siblings. If you're a BIPOC who has experienced racism *and* had access to certain educational and/or economic opportunities, you may feel survivor's guilt. You may also feel survivor's guilt if you've been successful in your life, as you may be very much aware that the majority of your community is struggling and facing high rates of destruction, poverty, and injustice. But survivor's guilt isn't limited to those BIPOC with more privilege. If you grew up in a neighborhood where you experienced high trauma, or if you've lost family and/or friends to racially motivated police brutality and mass incarceration, you may also experience survivor's guilt when you consider the fates of those who weren't so fortunate.

Another cause of survivor's guilt may include having benefited from colorism, discrimination against darker-complexioned BIPOC family and friends. *Colorism*, which is rooted in White supremacy, is the valuing of people who have more European features and lighter skin, and the simultaneous devaluing of darker-complexioned people. Colorism has historically and in contemporary times been demonstrated through disparities in numerous institutions, from the media to education to the criminal justice system (Blake et al. 2017; Hall 2018; Smart 2018). Unfortunately, colorism has been internalized by many BIPOC and is evident in disparities in treatment within families, BIPOC businesses, and even social gatherings. Lighter-complexioned BIPOC who are aware of the ways they have benefited from colorism may experience a level of guilt that some respond to with denial and others respond to with a sense of pressure to prove their commitment to racial justice, including justice for darker-complexioned BIPOC. Educator Dr. Jasmine Haywood (2017) shares this quote from an Afro-Latinx interviewee:

> *My mom would joke around and say she was going to bathe me in milk. One of the jokes she used to say when I asked why I was darker than everybody else was that she left me in the oven for too long. Yeah. So, growing up I always wanted to be lighter skinned and I found myself not attractive because I was dark skinned.*

An additional cause of guilt for BIPOC comes from an awareness of prejudice within themselves, their family, and/or their community against other racial/ethnic groups. The most pervasive form of prejudice among BIPOC is anti-Black prejudice. It aligns with the messaging, socialization, and societal hierarchy enforced by White supremacy, which places Blackness at the bottom of the social order; as a result, members of other BIPOC groups may try to distance themselves from the lower levels of the hierarchy by denigrating Black people and participating in their oppression. BIPOC may feel guilty for the ways they or their community has internalized White supremacy and believed, promoted, and acted on negative stereotypes about other BIPOC.

While anti-Asian racism has existed throughout US history, there was a rise in anti-Asian racism starting with the COVID-19 pandemic, in which political leaders used language that blamed Asians and sparked increased suspicion, rejection, and hostility toward Asian Americans and Pacific Islanders including physical assaults on elders and mass murder of Asian American women. While most Americans are familiar with the stereotype of Asian Americans as the "model minority," stories of Asian Americans' struggles have often been untold. The legalized oppression of Asians has included discriminatory immigration laws, internment camps, and deception around promises for citizenship that were not honored. The experiences of impoverished Asian Americans and South Asian Americans have been routinely erased.

Take a moment to describe any experience you've had with survivor's guilt as it relates to each of the following:

1. Feeling guilty about success and/or opportunities:

    _____

    _____

2. Feeling guilty about the widespread suffering of other members of your race:

    _____

    _____

3. Feeling guilty about colorism, anti-Black racism, and/or receiving preferential treatment compared to other BIPOC:

    _____

    _____

Now, how do you typically cope with these feelings when they arise? BIPOC cope with feelings of survivor's guilt in diverse ways. Some try to save everyone—and neglect themselves. Maybe you find that you comfort others while holding your own pain inside because you don't want to be a burden. Or maybe you're stretching your finances thin by trying to support loved ones beyond your capacity. Some of us may feel too guilty to enjoy good opportunities and resources that come our way. Others try to hide their accomplishments and feel embarrassed by what they have achieved. Some BIPOC end up lashing out at those who didn't emerge unscathed: they blame their family and community for "not trying harder" to achieve what they want in life. Some feel the need to constantly prove their authenticity and solidarity, to the point where it may be performative.

Survivor's guilt can result in depression, anxiety, a sense of isolation, and even imposter syndrome, or a feeling of not belonging in a space where one is the only one or one of a few people of their race. It's important to remember that imposter syndrome doesn't begin in the individual but is rooted in institutional racism, which by design, causes BIPOC to feel unwelcome and unacceptable. For example, when you're one of the few people of color in your job or university, remind yourself that the numbers are not reflective of the ability or intelligence of people from your race but are a result of bias, discrimination, and barriers to resources.

José is a Mexican American man living in Los Angeles. He is a married father of two with a moderately good income position. He is the first in his family to graduate from college and the rest of his family is struggling with weekly crises related to poverty, trauma, and immigration stress. In the past, José felt guilty for a relative who was deported and then killed. He also feels a lot of grief for the Latinx children who were separated from their parents and placed in cages on the border. He believes no one cares about his community and that he can't rest and enjoy his life while his community suffers. This guilt causes him to postpone vacations or only go places where he can afford to take his extended family with him. The guilt he feels also creates strain on his marriage and gives him social anxiety, as most people are not passionate about racial injustice as he is. The strain on the marriage manifests in his often struggling with depression and anger, which both create barriers to him seeing and attending to the emotional needs of his wife. His wife, who loves him dearly and shares his pain with what's happening to so many in their community, feels José takes on too much of what they struggle with himself in ways that are making his life and his family's lives harder.

You can see many of the effects of survivor's guilt at work in José's story. Fill in the following chart to raise your awareness regarding the effects survivor's guilt has had on you. You may want to first take a look at José's chart to help you begin thinking about your experiences and reactions.

Effects of Survivor's Guilt	My Feelings	My Thoughts	My Actions	My Relationships
In the Past	Depressed, guilty	I need to do more. I should have been able to protect my family, even when I was a child. I was the oldest and it was my responsibility.	Staying busy at work and with extended family. Perfectionism. No amount that I do is ever enough.	Relationships with extended family are strained. They depend on me, but resent me and accuse me of being controlling.
In the Present	Frustrated	I don't see how people can just go on with their lives and not care about the suffering that is happening right at this moment.	Smoking marijuana more to calm down and get some sleep.	My wife is exhausted and makes comments about feeling lonely even though I'm right here.

Effects of Survivor's Guilt	My Feelings	My Thoughts	My Actions	My Relationships
In the Past				
In the Present				

While some BIPOC cope in unhealthy ways, there are also those who feel motivated to work for racial justice while also giving themselves permission to experience joy, inner peace, and fulfillment. If survivor's guilt is something you've struggled with as a BIPOC, becoming more aware of it can help you move to solidarity, combined with self- and community-care. Living in solidarity with BIPOC from your and other races requires a recognition of what psychology researchers Drs. Christine Rosales and Regina Langhout (2020) call *offstage resistance* or *everyday resistance*. While attending protest marches and posting on social media can raise awareness and create important opportunities to demonstrate solidarity, it is critical for BIPOC to seek out and embrace support for the lives and liberties of all BIPOC through inclusion, advocacy, and affirmation. It's important to honor the work of protest, especially as journalist Jim Daley reported for *Scientific American* on a recent research study that found that cities with the most active Black Lives Matter (BLM) chapters saw a significant decrease in police killings of civilians. Specifically, the study found that there was up to a 20 percent decrease in killings by police in municipalities where BLM protests were held, resulting in an estimated three hundred fewer deaths nationwide from 2014 to 2019. Black Lives Matter protests increased the likelihood of police departments adopting body-worn cameras and community-policing initiatives. Many cities with larger and more frequent BLM protests experienced greater declines in police homicides.

In addition to the important work of protesting, there are also everyday acts of resistance that we invite you to consider adopting:

1. Engaging in self-care and mutual care within your community.

2. Celebrating your culture instead of surrendering to the pull to hide it or apologize for it.

3. Promote and recommend other BIPOC for opportunities that you become aware of.

4. Raise your children to be proud of and knowledgeable about their heritage.

5. Seek out community events where you feel a sense of belonging and connection.

6. Engage in cultural healing practices such as artistic or spiritual traditions that emerge from your community.

Above all, it's most crucial to remember that solidarity requires breaking silence and breaking ranks from White supremacy, which promotes division and competition between BIPOC.

As we consider the shift into solidarity, take a moment to consider the barriers that have kept you from practicing solidarity with other BIPOC groups in the past, and one way you can move forward. The following questions ask you to consider other BIPOC groups you have internalized stereotypes about, and how you can practice solidarity with members of those groups instead.

What is one negative stereotype you have about BIPOC of a different race or income level than you?

_____

_____

Where did you first learn that stereotype?

_____

_____

Who benefits from you holding that stereotype? Who suffers from you holding that stereotype?

_____

_____

What other races have you heard jokes or negative comments about? What were the statements?

_____

_____

What are some factors that made it hard to speak up in those moments to voice your disagreement?

_____

_____

Looking back on those moments, what would need to shift in you to allow you to speak up in solidarity?

_____

_____

What could you have said in the past? What will you say or do in the future?

_____

_____

Again, an important cognitive skill is reframing your perspective—in this case, shifting from perspectives that keep you trapped in guilt, and in racism, to perspectives that motivate you to change and correct the patterns of your past and to be actively antiracist. On the left in the chart below are common statements of BIPOC guilt—which many of us will say or think at one point or another, but can keep us stagnant or disconnected from the community. On the right, rewrite the statement with a reframe that allows you to free yourself from disconnection and survivor's guilt, while still standing in solidarity with other BIPOC. The first one is completed as an example.

Common Statements of BIPOC Guilt	Statement Reframe
I feel terrible about having a good life when I know so many other BIPOC are suffering.	I'm appreciative of the good things I have in life and I try to use the resources I have to create more opportunities and equity for others.
I don't feel I can share my good news when so many members of my community are having a hard time.	
I'm just not comfortable around Black people.	
I can't be an activist. I don't even have the courage to speak up when my family talks badly about other people of color.	
I really feel if we fight for the rights of other BIPOC, it will just end up with our community having less.	

Releasing immobilizing guilt requires moving into awareness or acknowledgment of our thoughts and behaviors, actively working toward shifting our attitudes, and then engaging in actions of solidarity. In the previous exercises, you've worked on awareness of privileges you hold and mistakes you may have made. It can also help to consider where our thoughts and fears came from. Often they are not products of our imagination. We have been taught by various sources to fear, judge, and mistrust others. To actively see this messaging and begin questioning it and recognizing it as a problem, as untruths, and as counterproductive to antiracism is critical for the work you've chosen to do.

As you reflect on where you are in your thinking and where these thoughts originate, we now invite you to consider your future—and more specifically, one thing you can do to better stand in solidarity with other BIPOC.

_____

_____

_____

Finally, it is important to acknowledge that for some BIPOC, guilt—for wrongs of the past they feel a deep need to fix, or from a sense that they're not doing enough—drives them to overextend themselves in antiracist work and neglect themselves and their health. If you fall into this category, setting boundaries and learning that you do not have to say yes to every request are important steps on the antiracism journey. If you overextend or ignore your body's alarm, which can lead to burnout and other health consequences, it is important to release your guilt in order to also release yourself from self-abandonment.

While you're fighting for the lives of others, your life matters too. Your wellness matters too. Losing sight of that fact can become another way that you're oppressed by racism; suddenly racism, a systemic problem, has become *your* problem alone to fix.

Meditate on these affirmations as you sit in a comfortable place:

My life matters.

My mental health matters.

My rest matters.

While working toward liberation, I will not participate in my own oppression.

I honor my right to breathe, to exist, and to flourish, not to the exclusion of others but also not to the exclusion of myself.

White People and Racism-Related Guilt

If you're White, the guilt you feel may be more collective in nature than it is individual. *Collective White guilt* refers to feelings of group-based guilt among White people resulting from the awareness that White people as a group have an illegitimate advantage over other groups, and that White people have caused harm to other racial groups, according to psychologists Drs. Allison Blodorn and Laurie O'Brien in their 2011 article. Often, when you become aware of your collective guilt as a White person, you may feel upset—you might think something like, I *didn't do this! I didn't cause harm!* I'm *not racist!* Sit with these feelings if they arise; see if you can let the knee-jerk reaction pass in order to let a more balanced understanding of your role and responsibility as a White person in a racist system—from which you benefit—emerge. Sitting with that reality can be a part of your motivation to engage, instead of an often-automatic defensiveness that can lead to disengagement. Even as you read (and maybe reread) this paragraph, we invite you to breathe deeply and give yourself sacred pause for reflection.

It's understandable to feel this amorphous, global sort of guilt. But collective White guilt is ultimately a self-focused response to injustice as opposed to other-focused responses you could have such as sympathy and anger. It's also associated with higher mental distress than other-focused responses such as sympathy and anger, which often motivate the person feeling them to seek and express emotional justice for those who've been wronged. If, as a White person, you find that you often recognize that acts of racism have occurred and feel collective White guilt, you might experience negative mental health consequences such as depression, anxiety, and somatic complaints like migraines. This relationship between White guilt and negative mental health consequences was found in studies examining racism and the response to Hurricane Katrina. An additional potential negative consequence is becoming immobilized by excessive guilt. Because the guilt you feel is for being a member of your race—something you can't really control, and something you may never have had to confront in the same way that many BIPOC do every day—it may come to seem like a fact of the world that you, as a person, can't do anything but lament. Or, conversely, you may find that sometimes you're thankful for the privileges that being White gives you, relative to other races, and that in turn becomes a source of guilt. The following quote comes from an article published in 2001 by educator Dr. Jan Arminio, entitled "Exploring the Nature of Race-Related Guilt."

> Elizabeth: *"So, I feel like a light bulb has gone on for me. I grew up not having to think about being White very often… Today I think about being White all the time. Sometimes I feel guilty, sometimes I feel thankful. Then I feel guilty for feeling thankful."*

Whatever the nature of the guilt you feel, the desire to avoid guilt and psychological distress may serve as an incentive for you or other White people you know to deny that racism exists, is pervasive, and has consequences in others' lives and in your own.

But as psychological research makes clear, for antiracist engagement to persist, the goal is not to avoid guilt altogether but to use guilt as a spur to shift from excessive, overwhelming distress to a sense of responsibility and agency that motivates individual and collective antiracism action. In other words, you need to learn to tolerate the distress you feel around privilege and collective White guilt—and then use that distress as motivation to behave in ways that challenge and disrupt racism as it operates in the world around you. Viewed in this light, the guilt that you feel about racism as a White person can serve as a motivator to engage in antiracist behaviors including supporting racial justice policies, speaking up for BIPOC, and leveraging your privilege for good in your life, your community, and the world. In fact, when Whites perceive racism and feel collective guilt, but then engage in antiracism acts, they benefit psychologically through a decrease in emotional distress, according to psychologists Dr. Blodorn and O'Brien. In this way, your commitment to antiracism can motivate your participation in social justice and your activity can benefit your mental health. And ultimately, when justice for all is your goal, your journey is not just to alleviate guilt, or even only to unlearn racist attitudes that you've been taught or exposed to but also to commit to corrective action to dismantle racial oppression.

In that spirit, if you're a White person feeling racism-related guilt or discomfort, a helpful tool might be liberation psychology, which is all about moving from distress or disconnection to antiracist action, with the goal of our collective liberation from racism. If you feel guilty and/or shame about specific things you've done or not done, it is important to acknowledge the impact of your actions or inaction, or of the actions others have taken that you feel guilt or shame for, and to make amends through not only remorse but also unlearning racism, learning antiracism, and actively participating in the work for racial justice.

Remember, it is important to acknowledge your guilt and the source of it.

Describe below the guilt or discomfort you feel about one historical act of racism.

_____

_____

_____

_____

_____

_____

Describe below the guilt or discomfort you feel when you reflect on your privilege as a White person and how it's benefited you, or when you reflect on a specific action or lack of action you've taken related to racism.

_____

_____

_____

_____

_____

_____

_____

Now that you've acknowledged these feelings and incidents, it's important to begin thinking about ways that you can choose responsible engagement over stagnant guilt.

Along with working on yourself through this workbook, list three things that you have done or can do to combat racism and/or promote racial justice.

1. _____

_____

2. _____

_____

3. _____

_____

While the things you've done or can do may seem small to you, as you think about the global reality of racism, remember that each of us can make a difference by shifting the tide from racism to antiracism, from racial oppression to racial justice. The work you do as an individual doesn't stop with you. It ripples outward and changes the world around you—sometimes in ways you may not even be aware of.

So, visualize yourself working for racial justice as part of a long line of people, historically and in the present, doing their part. Hold the image in your mind, place your hands on your heart if that aligns with you, and take a cleansing breath.

Megan's Journey

Megan is a cisgender White woman in her late forties, and while she has always been bothered by racism, she never felt equipped to do anything about it. When she would read about racism, learn about issues on the news, or hear friends talk about it, she felt a sinking feeling in her stomach. Her heart felt heavy as she thought about her inaction and the likely involvement of her ancestors in racist systems like slavery. One year, she attended a professional conference and heard a Black woman speaking about how racism was not Black people's problem to solve but how everyone has a responsibility to combat it.

Megan felt shame and guilt for her years of silence, but then felt motivated to do something. She sent out an email to her White friends to see if anyone wanted to join her in forming a book club to learn about racism and how to fight it. While a number of people didn't respond, a few said yes and their group began. The group has now been running for five years and not only do they read books together but they also engage in different calls to action such as fundraising, attending protests, boycotting companies with racist policies, and donating books on racism to schools.

Reminder: you can find a book club guide for *this* book here: http://www.newharbinger.com/49104.

Liberating Ourselves from Immobilizing Guilt

As we conclude this chapter, the following is an embodied healing activity to help you shift from excessive guilt to inspired racial justice activism. Though change occurs on the cognitive, or mental, level, there's also a way in which guilt lives in the body—so shifting that deeper level of guilt requires us to engage the body.

1. Imagine guilt as a heavy load and spend a few minutes exploring what it feels like to carry that load. Experiment with how you move when your head is weighed down, or your back, your arms, or your legs. See what it feels like to move slowly or to buckle under the burden of excessive guilt.

2. After you've spent some time moving with the heavy load of guilt, consider how much additional time and effort would be required to do anything including the work of racial justice.

3. Now imagine the weight of guilt being in your hands as a heavy load, but then shifting to a flame in your head and heart. This flame inspires you to think, feel, and act for racial justice. Begin moving around with the flame within you. Experiment with how it feels to be inspired to act. How does your head feel and move? How do your arms, back, and legs move when you're free to flow in sync with the inner flame, the inner value of racial justice?

4. After you've spent a few minutes moving in this way, reflect on what it would feel like to shift from the load of excessive guilt to the flame of inspired, value-based living. We invite you to give yourself permission to make that shift, still very much aware of racial injustice, but no longer stuck in guilt about it—free to activate.

CHAPTER 6

Challenging Victim-Blaming and Respectability Politics: Moving Past Stereotypes and Biases

Maybe you've heard the phrases *victim-blaming* and *respectability politics*. If you're familiar with the terms, you may wonder what they have to do with each other. When it comes to experiences with racism, both victim-blaming (when we blame the people who experience racism for somehow bringing that experience on themselves) and respectability politics (when we believe we can avoid the racism directed at our particular racial group by behaving in the "appropriate ways") rely on stereotypes about racial groups. Far too often, race-based stereotypes shape how we expect people to behave and how we think people deserve to be treated based on their racial group membership. And when we fall into this trap, whether as White people or as BIPOC, we aid and abet racism rather than confronting and challenging it.

We will state clearly at the outset of this chapter: Targets or victims of racism are not responsible for experiencing racism. That responsibility lies solely with its perpetrators. If you're a Black or Indigenous person, or other person of color, the racism you or other BIPOC experience is not the result of anything you do. And to assume that it is—even if you think it's in the service of your survival—is to play into racism. In this chapter, we're going to take a closer look at race-based stereotypes and how they play out in victim-blaming and respectability politics. We'll also explore how stereotypes, victim-blaming, and respectability politics are all roadblocks to challenging racism and will offer suggestions on how to navigate these roadblocks on the way to cultivating antiracist practice.

Let's start with stereotypes and why they're such a threat to authentic interactions and relationships, within and across racial groups.

Stereotypes as Threats

Stereotypes occur when certain attributes—positive or negative—are associated with various social groups. Social psychological researchers have examined how race-status associations serve as a specific type of stereotype where, for example, White Americans are given a higher status and other racial groups, such as Black Americans, are assigned a lower status (Dupree, Torrez, Obioha, and Fiske 2020).

Think back to our discussion of racial hierarchy in American history and how this culture advantages White people, with Black people, Indigenous people, and other people of color assigned lesser value. When we think of race-based stereotypes in the context of the racial hierarchy, we can see how positive attributes have come to be associated with higher status on that hierarchy and negative attributes with lower status. For example, when BIPOC navigate professional settings, stereotypes about what's "attractive" or "desirable" will influence how they feel they are able to present themselves in terms of how they wear their hair or whether they feel they can wear clothing that represents their cultural background without being judged negatively or penalized for it. Or think about the language you've heard used to describe White youth who are charged with crimes as compared to BIPOC youth. Often, when BIPOC youth are described, it will be with language that implies some essential criminality or some flaw in their background or family circumstance. White youth, on the other hand, are often humanized, with language that speaks to their supposed virtues or what unlikely perpetrators they seem to be.

Take a moment to reflect on stereotypes that you've encountered as a member of the racial group(s) with which you identify. Respond to the following questions by writing your answers in the spaces provided below:

While growing up, what stereotypes about *your racial group(s)* do you remember learning about from your family? School? Media?

_____

_____

How did it make you feel when you encountered stereotypes about your racial group(s)? Did it make a difference if the stereotypes were positive or negative?

_____

_____

While growing up, what stereotypes *about other racial group(s)* do you remember learning about from your family? School? Media?

_____

_____

Were you able to talk with friends or family when you encountered stereotypes about your racial group(s)? Or other racial groups? What messages do you remember taking away from these conversations that helped you understand what was going on?

_____

_____

Have stereotypes you've learned about your own racial group(s) or others' affected your behavior in adulthood? How?

_____

_____

It's important that we reflect on the stereotypes we've encountered about our racial group(s), because it helps us to make sense of our experiences and, hopefully, learn that stereotypes do not define who we are as individuals or how we should feel about our sense of worth. Although we may believe we are not personally affected by race-based stereotypes that are not about our groups, or we may find ourselves benefiting from stereotypes that advantage our groups, it's still important that we take action to confront them. Far too often, inaction in the face of stereotypes can serve to affirm or confirm those stereotypes, which are then used to justify negative treatment of disadvantaged groups.

Unfortunately, we know that stereotypes can be used to justify people acting on their prejudices to discriminate against other people. And most often, those discriminated against are members of lower-status groups such as racially disadvantaged communities. Just as families use racial socialization to prepare youth to be able to navigate and challenge racism they experience, being able to recognize stereotyping when it occurs can help targets of stereotypes to confront and reject these dynamics.

Members of groups who are stereotyped against do not need to accept or internalize the stereotypes about their group to be negatively impacted. *Stereotype threat* occurs when people act with the awareness of a certain stereotype "in the air," leading the person to fear they will confirm the stereotype in some way, which can then have a negative impact on how they perform in academic, athletic, or professional arenas (Rios, Case, Brody, and Rivera 2021; Steele, 1997).

The extent to which we believe negative stereotypes about our own or other racial groups can shape how we view people's behavior and how we think people should be treated. We see this dynamic at play when we try to make sense of racism that we personally experience or that others experience. While we hope that we would respond with the empathy and support that people deserve when they experience racism, sometimes we fall short. As a result, we end up blaming the targets of racism and failing to hold the perpetrators of racism accountable. Let's look at two examples of this dynamic—victim-blaming and respectability politics—and how we can challenge ourselves to counter those dynamics as a way to practice antiracism.

CHALLENGING VICTIM-BLAMING AND REJECTING RESPECTABILITY POLITICS

When it comes to race and racism, victim-blaming occurs when we look at the racial disparities that exist in our country, such as the disproportionate numbers of Black and Indigenous people and people of color who contend with chronic illnesses or live in lower-income neighborhoods, and believe that these circumstances exist because of some moral failing of BIPOC communities. Or when people who are BIPOC experience racism and think it was their fault because they supposedly displayed some behavior that fulfilled a negative race-based stereotype.

Let's take a moment to reflect on some of the victim-blaming stereotypes that exist for the challenges facing various BIPOC groups. You might think about the underrepresentation of BIPOC at elite colleges and universities. Or the disproportionate rates of incarceration for Black and Brown people. Too often, people hold beliefs about why such disparities exist that do not focus on societal inequities but instead make the situation that particular BIPOC community's problem or fault. So in the case of college admissions, people may endorse stereotypes about intelligence to explain the underrepresentation of BIPOC in the student body instead of examining the privileges that being a member of an advantaged racial or socioeconomic group might provide in the admissions process.

There are many biases we may hold, consciously and unconsciously, that can be used to explain inequitable outcomes for BIPOC that are actually rooted in racism. Accepting stereotypes about groups can keep us from engaging, to be a part of the solution, because we believe the people affected just need to behave better. Additionally, blaming targets of racism shifts our focus from the systemic and structural nature of racism to that of an individual failing by those who experience racism.

Think about any number of recent cases of police brutality that have been highlighted in the media. How often have you heard a media personality, politician, or even a family member or friend attempt to justify police brutality by blaming the victim in a way that perpetuates negative race-based stereotypes (such as false beliefs about the propensity for violent behavior in racially disadvantaged communities)? We'll reiterate here: Blaming targets of racism for the racism they experience shifts responsibility from perpetrators to victims. Since victim-blaming is something that people who are BIPOC and people who are White do, it is up to all of us to challenge victim-blaming and move toward antiracist practice.

EXERCISE: Challenging Victim-Blaming

Let's flex those critical consciousness skills we started to develop in chapter 2 ("Educating Yourself") and interrogate our awareness and acceptance of negative race-based stereotypes.

- Think back to a time that you learned about a racist experience someone else had, and instead of empathizing with the target of racism, you questioned what the target could have done to warrant that experience.

- Stop right there and ask yourself: "What negative race-based stereotype am I relying on to blame this person for the racism they experienced?"

- Recognize that at this moment you're moving from believing a stereotype and using it to justify racism to questioning the stereotype. *This is a good thing and represents progress in moving toward antiracist practice.*

- Now challenge yourself to move from questioning the stereotype to rejecting it as a rationale for someone being racially discriminated against.

In the future, when incidents of racism come up, either in the national news or in your own community and life, try to use this process of reflection as you continue to confront race-based stereotypes as a way to challenge victim-blaming in response to racism.

Rejecting Respectability Politics

Respectability politics arise when we accept race-based stereotypes of our own and other groups, which in turn influences the ways we view ourselves and how we navigate social interactions. It all begins when we internalize negative stereotypes about those groups who are disadvantaged by the American racial hierarchy and affirm positive stereotypes about groups higher on the racial hierarchy. We then attempt to navigate racism by acting as if members of racially disadvantaged groups could somehow avoid experiencing racism if they acted in ways that are stereotypically associated with the higher-status racial group.

The lie and illusion of respectability promote the idea that, for instance, if you dress "nicely," wear your hair in ways that mirror Eurocentric standards, speak softly, follow all police commands without question, speak "proper English," and do what you're told, then you won't be harmed by racism. In many respects, respectability politics has been a survival strategy for racially disadvantaged groups over time to attempt to avoid the most harmful ramifications of living in a racially stratified society where the lives of Black people, Indigenous people, and people of color have been threatened by overt acts of racist violence.

But respectability is of limited utility as a coping strategy because of the power dynamics and reality of racism. Racism cannot be justified by the use of any race-based stereotypes. People from racially disadvantaged communities are not responsible for racism because their behavior confirms a race-based stereotype. Those who perpetrate racism are the ones responsible for it. What's more, if you're Black or Indigenous, or another person of color who has consciously structured your self-presentation and your behavior in ways that defy stereotypes to avoid being mistreated, this strategy may not save you from the effects of racism. Remember that racism operates at multiple levels. And racism as a system is bigger than individual discriminatory actions, which means that as individuals who experience racist actions from others, we cannot depend on respectability politics to insulate us from racism. Only the antiracist actions we take to confront racism across the levels that it is expressed— whether individually, culturally, or systemically—will bring about the change we hope to see. Ultimately, it is in all of our best interests to challenge the racial hierarchy that creates and reinforces stereotypes about racial groups and to refuse to measure ourselves and others against these stereotypes. We make progress toward an antiracist society by rejecting the racial hierarchy and refusing to validate racist stereotypes that are meant to keep us from living as fully and freely as possible.

The Mindful Moment below offers several ways to release the burden of being constrained by race-based stereotypes.

MINDFUL MOMENT: *That Burden Is Not Mine to Carry*

Visualize the weight that stereotypes lay on you. How do you feel when you think about what others say you're supposed to be (or cannot be) or are allowed to do (or not do) because of your racial group membership?

Visualize yourself laying that weight down. Or picture your ancestors lifting that weight from you. Tell yourself: *That burden is not mine to carry. I am returning to sender. I am letting go of all of the baggage that does not have my name.*

Visualize members of a different racial group and imagine the stereotypes that you've internalized about them as a curtain. Be intentional about removing the curtain and seeing people for the first time without stereotypes, fears, and assumptions.

We hope this chapter illuminated that, whether it is victim-blaming or engaging in respectability politics, race-based stereotypes must be challenged and questioned. Again, our beliefs about how members of racial groups should behave or be treated have been shaped by a racial hierarchy that advantages some groups and disadvantages others. When we place the blame for racism on those who experience it instead of those who perpetrate it, we are part of the problem.

To become part of the solution, we must commit to challenging race-based stereotypes by questioning and then rejecting them in ourselves and in the behaviors and actions of others. This begins the process of removing the responsibility for stereotypes or racism from those who are directly impacted by them and places the responsibility where it belongs: with the perpetrator.

CHAPTER 7

Confronting Fear: Just Do It

In a racist society, it is not enough to be non-racist, we must be antiracist.

—Angela Davis

When we are honest, we can acknowledge that one of the barriers that has prevented some antira-cism engagement is fear. Fear is a natural human emotion that is designed to alert you to danger and warn you to take protective action to keep yourself from being harmed. It can also come to obstruct your efforts to be antiracist in your life and actions when it's unfounded—more the result of your insecurities and projections than reality—or when it's intense and overwhelming, as it can often be when you're speaking up in a way you're not used to.

In this chapter, we will examine some of the specific things you may be afraid of and look at ways to confront those fears not only in your thinking but also in your personal relationships and in the larger world around you. We'll explore how you can get in touch with what fear feels like in your body and mind and learn to work with these sensations, rather than succumbing to them. We'll also look at how you can confront fear in antiracist work: of backlash (for BIPOC and White people alike), of the loss of privilege and the comforts of staying "neutral" in a racist system (for White people and privileged BIPOC), and of the potential to make mistakes in antiracist work (which can affect anyone doing any kind of antiracist work), rather than letting these fears control you.

To develop and activate an antiracist mindset, you must be prepared to confront your fears with a mindset in which you're aware of racism and willing to confront it and work to disrupt it. As you think about being vocally and visibly antiracist, consider the fears that come to mind. Consider how you've seen other people who were engaged in antiracism efforts treated or talked about. It's impor-tant for you to be prepared for the possibilities of what may occur—people criticizing you, disagreeing with you, questioning your actions, motives, or efficacy; tension and stress from situations you might find yourself in; and personal and professional consequences from the antiracist actions you take—because if you're not prepared, you may be shocked and quickly decide it is not worth it for you to honor your commitment to antiracism.

Let's begin by looking at what fear feels like in our bodies when it arises so you know what to look for—and how to deal with it in ways that are healthy and effective.

EXERCISE: Imagining Your Activism

Imagine yourself engaging in an antiracism action that you've yet to participate in. You may visualize yourself:

- Attending a march or protest

- Posting an antiracist message on social media

- Challenging a family member or friend who commonly makes racist comments

- Speaking up about racial inequities in your job, organization, or faith community and demanding action be taken

As you see yourself engaging in this action, think about what you feel, physically and emotionally. What emotions arise in your body and in your mind?

What did you feel doing the visualization? It might've been excitement, the satisfaction of acting in ways aligned with your values, and the fulfillment of making a difference. You may feel the inclusion of belonging with a community of antiracism activists.

On the other hand, you may also feel tense and afraid. Some physical signs of fear are:

- Heart-racing

- Sweating

- Dry mouth

- Chest pains

- Shortness of breath

- Trembling

- Upset stomach

- Chest pains

You might also experience racing thoughts or a sense of panic at the risk you're about to take or the ways others might respond. Know that all of this is normal. *And,* if we judge ourselves for being afraid, we often intensify our distress.

Here, as always, the key is to develop the ability to tolerate the distress that will arise any time you take courageous antiracist action—specifically, by cultivating acceptance of and compassion for the fear you feel. If you have some fear about taking action and speaking up about racism, you're not alone. Researchers who examined antiracism dialogue in schools noted that besides denial and guilt, fear can be a major barrier in antiracism engagement for teachers (Flintoff and colleagues 2015).

Compassion and Acceptance of Your Fear: Breathe

It may help you to know that great activists who you may admire were not always fearless—but were courageous despite their fears.

Rosa Parks took action in the civil rights movement despite fear of arrest and other potential consequences. She refused to give up her seat on a bus for a White person, although the law and the bus driver were against her. She was an active organizer and activist who was initiating a larger plan to launch a bus boycott in protest of the unjust busing policies discriminating against Black people. In reflecting on her antiracism engagement and the engagement of others, Rosa Parks said, "I have learned over the years that when one's mind is made up, this diminishes fear; knowing what must be done does away with fear."

We hope, as you read this chapter, that you make up your mind that the work of antiracism must be done and that you choose to be a part of that work. As you commit, the fear may not disappear, but we hope it will diminish so that it doesn't overshadow your values for racial justice.

When you feel afraid about initiating or deepening your antiracism engagement, give yourself the gift of radical acceptance, recognizing that fear is a human emotion and you're a human being. To show yourself compassion and acceptance, while also trying to regulate your fear, consider your breath as medicine. Often, rapid breathing is a potential symptom of distress—but the breath is also fundamental to our life; it keeps us alive, sustains us, and can even nourish us. Your breath can also be a place of healing and empowerment. (For those of you who are trauma survivors, tuning into the breath for an extended period of time can be triggering, so we encourage you to use caution by first taking a few breaths and seeing how that feels before you continue with longer breath focus. Even if taking one intentional cleansing breath seems like your limit, that one breath can be calming.)

When you feel afraid about activating or reactivating your antiracism efforts, we invite you to tap into your mind and thoughts and observe what arises. Try to simply notice your feelings, thoughts, body sensations, images, or memories as nonjudgmentally as you can. As you sit and simply observe what comes up for you, you'll likely experience a calming effect as the thoughts become disentangled.

As you breathe, you may want to clear your mind, or you want to focus on these affirmations:

- I breathe in courage and breathe out fear.

- I breathe in self-compassion and breathe out self-judgment.

- I breathe in acceptance of my humanity and breathe out perfectionism.

Understanding the Fear Response

When your body and brain receive the message of potential danger—for instance, when you stand up to speak at a new antiracist organization you've just joined and everyone turns in unison to look at you, or when you're at a protest or antiracist action and law enforcement arrives—it may trigger an automatic response. It might help you to connect with any times you felt anger, bitterness, frustration, and even outrage about the continuous trauma of racism. While your feelings are understandable and even a healthy response to outrageous events, given the prevalence of racism and the pain it causes, it can also be draining, unsustainable, and ineffective to feel emotionally overwhelmed and stuck in the outrage.

Another fear response is flight, to get away from the danger. In antiracism work, this will look like attending one march, making one post, engaging in one heated dialogue, attending one program or meeting, and then, when tensions arise as a result, leaving and never showing up again.

Freezing is yet another fear response. When you freeze, you're still physically present, but you're emotionally shut down. In antiracism work, this may manifest as being involved in an organization or attending events, but never speaking up, not allowing yourself to feel or express feelings when they arise or going through the motions—attending meetings, exchanging pleasantries, and doing the tasks you're invited or assigned to do—but feeling empty and disconnected from the community.

Another example of a fear response is "tend and befriend," which is when you shift into people-pleasing behaviors toward the person or people whom you identify as having power in the hopes that they will like you and keep you safe. In antiracism work, this can show up as idealizing leaders of antiracism organizations, rather than seeing them both appreciatively and realistically; or, as a White person, idealizing BIPOC rather than seeing them as real people with both virtues and flaws, whom you can have genuine relationships with; or, as a BIPOC, catering to White people in your antiracism work to the point of losing sight of yourself, being inauthentic (e.g., saying things you think might please a more privileged person, rather than speaking to how you really feel; deferring to them rather than speaking up and voicing your own ideas or needs), and being afraid to set boundaries (for instance, letting a White person or a more privileged BIPOC know that you don't in fact have time to work on an effort they're trying to recruit you for) for fear of being rejected.

Psychologist Dr. Jacqueline Nelson (2015) found in a study that many people are even hesitant to use the words "racism" and "antiracism." This reluctance is based in a fear that using the words will cause others to respond with defensiveness, sensitivity, or emotionally charged ways, so other more palatable words are often used. In light of this, simply naming racism and your commitment to antiracism can be a courageous act of resisting denial and avoidance.

The aim is to be aware of these fear responses and what may elicit them, so you can overcome the fears and live in ways that are congruent with your antiracism values.

In addition to the fears that can show up on the immediate, interpersonal level, there are also larger-scale fears that emerge in antiracist work. You may have the fear of failure to attain racial justice. You may be afraid that you'll commit time, energy, and effort to this work and it won't make a difference. This fear may lead to avoidance of antiracism dialogue or action steps due to a desire to avoid the disappointment of seeing racism continue or even increase over time. We can also frame this as fear of the unknown.

To some extent, fear of the unknown is both inevitable and justified. There are no guarantees in antiracism work. We cannot promise you that if we all do these specific things, racism will be dismantled, never to rise again. The reality is that we're not guaranteed to see the rewards of antiracist work in our lifetimes. We have to become comfortable planting seeds that future generations will hopefully see harvested, even if we don't. As Dr. King noted, "I may not get there with you but we as a people will get to the promised land."

So why should you engage in an effort that does not have guaranteed results? Here are two cognitive reframes to help you shift from the fear of ineffectiveness to the motivation for engagement.

1. You gain the opportunity to live in alignment with your values. While you cannot control what others will do, you have agency and accountability for what you choose to do. If you believe racial justice is important, then you want to live in such a way that you believe you did all you could do to attain it. When our actions are incongruent with our values or out of alignment, this can create distress, shame, guilt, and a sense of powerlessness. But when our actions reflect what we value, this sustains us, even in those times when our actions don't have the effects we might have hoped for. So, despite the unknown outcome, you can choose to speak and act in a way that reflects what you think and feel about racial justice. And if you do this, even the moments when you might not succeed will be worth it.

2. You can cultivate the ability to perceive small victories, instead of overlooking progress and therefore drowning in a sense of meaninglessness. Often, when we're trying to change some aspect of the way we live, we are looking for the big a-ha moments and major achievements, and we miss the mini awakenings and the little successes that happen along the way. In therapy, the therapist helps the client see even small bits of progress, which builds the confidence they need to continue on their wellness journey. And yes, the big goal in your antiracist work is to dismantle racism—but to be encouraged to continue the work, your eye has to be trained to see the wins along the way. If your child's school has never had a Black History Month program to spread awareness of the struggles Black people have faced in this country and the movements that helped achieve the civil rights victories they won, and as a result of your advocacy and organizing, they have their first program this year, that is a win. If your family member stops using racial slurs—even if it's just in your presence—that is a win. If your job begins to recruit more diverse applicants as a result of your efforts, that is a win. If you raise your child to see the beauty and pride of their culture as a BIPOC youth or to think critically about and challenge White supremacy as a White youth, that is a win. None of these wins are possible if we let the fear of the unknown stop our antiracist work.

It's also true that the work of coping with fear and uncertainty is not all on you as an individual. It can also be done in communities that you join and build.

Coping with Fear through Community

Healthy social support, also known as community support, can empower you to face your fears. Being antiracist alone can be overwhelming. It can be emotionally, socially, and politically helpful to connect with or build an antiracism community. These may be informal networks like your friends, family, and coworkers, or you might find formal groups and organizations to join. There are small local organizations and also larger national and even international organizations and conferences that aim to engage antiracism and work toward racial justice. You might even choose to create a new organization of your own if there isn't one in your area that fits what you're looking for.

Whatever form it takes, an antiracist social support network can provide you support on emotional, informational, instrumental, or tangible levels. Your network can give you people to whom you can express the sadness, fear, outrage, and fatigue you might feel about racism and antiracism work. It can let you know about opportunities to learn and engage in collective antiracism actions as they arise. Finally, your network can help you increase the impact you make with your antiracist work—by pooling your finances, signatures, networks, and votes, as opposed to just working by yourself as an individual.

What does your community look like now? Do you know people in your family or friend circles who share your commitment to antiracism in their thoughts, speech, and actions, and in what they do in their neighborhoods and the worlds around them? How might you like to better utilize the network around you, or expand it? To reflect on these possibilities, fill out the following table:

Names of my friends who are antiracist	
Names of my family members who are antiracist	
Names of people I work or go to school with who are antiracist	
An antiracism organization I have heard of (if you haven't heard of any, look online now and find one group whose work interests you and makes you feel you can contribute to it)	
An antiracism organization I am a member of or have attended a meeting or program sponsored by	

Now that you've written down some people and organizations you'd like to make part of your network, it's time to reach out. As you review the entries in your table, consider who you might want to collaborate with and when, depending on where you are in your own antiracist efforts. Is there someone on your list you want to reach out to now, to talk to them about the work you've been doing and want to do? Is there someone on your list you'd trust with your honest feelings and struggles as your antiracist efforts continue? How might you enlist this person in your efforts to be antiracist in your actions and resilient in your body and spirit? And the antiracist organizations you wrote down: Do you want to deepen your connection and commitment to the work they do? How?

How will I begin or continue building my antiracist support network?

_____

_____

_____

_____

_____

Now that we've discussed building a community for you to lean on when your antiracism gets intense, we're going to move on to what your support network can help you navigate—the fears that can arise as a result of the *effects* antiracist work can have: judgment from others, and labeling by others (as "angry," "problematic," "aggressive," "a troublemaker").

FEARS OF BACKLASH AND GETTING LABELED

You may fear being misunderstood or negatively labeled when you confront racism. Specifically, you may have concerns about people labeling you as angry, problematic, aggressive, or divisive. These labels often lead to various consequences: socially (not being invited to social outings with people who prefer to avoid discussing racism), professionally (not being promoted by supervisors who resent your calls for organizational change), academically (getting a negative grade on an assignment that addresses racism when graded by a professor who endorses racist ideologies), and politically (being targeted by voter suppression initiatives). These fears may be rooted in direct experiences of consequences you've suffered in the past—times you were chastised for speaking out in some way or making your presence as a BIPOC person known, or even punished in a material way, like losing certain privileges or titles at your job, or even your job itself. Or they may stem from times you've observed other people enduring these consequences as a result of brave choices they made. This may have led you to the belief that silence regarding racism is the safer, wiser choice. And even now, in the midst of your antiracism journey, these beliefs might be obstructing antiracist actions you're taking.

Of course, the fears aren't entirely unfounded. Let's be honest about some of these potential costs or consequences. Review the consequences listed in the table below and check off the ones you've experienced, either directly or vicariously. We have provided open spaces for you to add any other consequences to engaging in antiracism.

Potential Consequences	Check if you've experienced this	Check if you've seen or heard about this happening to others
Being isolated or avoided		
Being passed over for opportunities/jobs/promotions		
Being ridiculed/harassed		
Being shamed or chastised		
Receiving a poor grade or evaluation		
Being subject to rumors or gossip		

One of the strategies that can be helpful in addressing specific fears around backlash is picturing the worst thing happening and then visualizing yourself getting through it. Because this is something fear can keep you from understanding or being able to believe: you can in fact navigate loss and pain, even when it's intense; you can survive many of the things that scare you.

EXERCISE: Facing Your Fear

Imagine yourself speaking up about racism and then see yourself facing rejection from people in your family or job whom you know are racist, or are supportive of racism in direct and indirect ways. Take a breath and see yourself surviving their rejection. See yourself grieving those potential lost connections.

Next, see yourself building new relationships that are based in the shared value of racial justice and equity. In the face of these consequences, visualize your options. You may want to see yourself speaking up about the backlash. You may visualize yourself filing a complaint. You may visualize yourself walking away. You may visualize yourself talking to a supportive friend, creating artwork, or engaging in a spiritual practice.

There can be empowerment in seeing yourself building a full life, even with the consequences of being antiracist in a racist society.

Below, describe the consequence you visualized and how you saw yourself getting through it.

_____

_____

_____

_____

_____

White Privilege and Fear

As you learned in the introductory chapters, the myth of White superiority promotes the idea that White people by virtue of their race are more moral, intelligent, kind, worthy, and beautiful than people of color. For our White readers, when you engage in antiracism—no longer sitting silent when you hear someone say or do something racist, suggesting ways that your family, work, or day-to-day environments may be more equitable and respectful of BIPOC, and pointing out racist ideas and behaviors you see in your community—you may lose some of the benefits automatically bestowed on Whites by other White people. White people who either openly promote racial injustice or deny the existence of racial injustice will be angry about your stance. They will feel betrayed by you and may become hostile or even reject you, socially, politically, or professionally. Silence buys you a free pass to enjoy White privilege uninterrupted and unchallenged. To become vocal about antiracism is to be willing to face rejection and penalty from people in your life who are invested in protecting the status quo, which is racism.

You'll need to ask yourself if you've decided your values and the lives of BIPOC are worth the costs you might incur. Silence is a choice. Engagement is a choice. Either way, you're choosing how to respond to racism. In making this choice, it may help you to consider not just your fears of loss or being targeted because you stand against racism but what your silence has cost and what it might cost in the future. Are there relationships you've had to sacrifice because you weren't willing to confront your own privilege? Is there a mental or emotional burden you carry because of the privilege you hold, which antiracist work could help lighten? If you were to let go of any commitment to antiracism, what would your life and the lives of people you care about look like? How would you feel about yourself?

To gain motivation and courage to step forward despite the cost, please complete the following exercise. You'll see we've also included examples from Alice, a White woman who stayed silent even though she suspects the recent layoff of a colleague on her team at work was racially motivated since other White members of the team who were less accomplished weren't targeted.

My silence about racial injustice has cost me:	My silence about racial injustice has cost BIPOC:
The trust of a good friend when I didn't speak up for her	Potentially, a job—if I had spoken up about the racist implications of what was happening, my friend might not have been let go

As you count the cost of inaction on your well-being and the greater well-being of BIPOC, we hope you'll make the decision that the cost of silence is too high and you're ready to move forward in antiracism practice.

BIPOC and Fear of Loss

BIPOC antiracism activists have faced social and material consequences for their work, and even physical danger, and this is a reality that may understandably cause a lot of fear for you. In the way we often tell history, the danger that activists confront is minimized; it may be presented as a one-off, rare, or an injustice that only occasionally happens. Also, it's sometimes painted as having been caused by outliers, frustrated individual racists, even though individual racist actors are produced by racist systems and abetted by those who subscribe to these systems. For instance, we are all well aware of the assassination of Dr. Martin Luther King, Jr. Most people are less aware of the retaliation, surveillance, harassment, and harm done to contemporary antiracism activists, especially those working to address anti-Blackness. What's more, the fears that those of us who are aware of these realities have are heightened because they do not just include fear of random "counterprotestors" who might derail and sabotage protest movements, but also fear of state-sanctioned retributive violence by police or other governmental agencies. And of course, there are the reprisals faced by people who don't define themselves as activists but merely take day-to-day antiracism action and end up with such consequences as losing a job, being harassed online, or being arrested at protests or voter mobilization events.

In Ferguson, Michael Brown, an African American man, was killed and his body was left lying in the street for more than four hours. According to Jackson and Welles (2016), Black community members went to social media and shared how his murder, exposed body, and subsequent suspicious murders of several antiracism activists left them with immense confusion, outrage, and fear. Creating fear in racially marginalized community members has long been a tool of racism to attempt to silence, suppress, and immobilize marginalized people. We and others would refer to this as domestic terrorism, the terrorizing of a people to render them powerless.

First, we want you to know that being afraid of physical harm and incarceration are natural fears and concerns that you do not need to be ashamed of. Yes, people have put their lives and bodies on the line for racial justice. *And* each of us needs to make an individual decision about the level of risk we're willing to take.

For those who choose to engage in direct action or protest that makes your identity visible, we encourage you to engage within an organization that provides training on strategies to stay safe—staying with the group, only engaging in predetermined action, or having someone who is not present but knows where you are. Also, ideally, they will inform you about what to do in cases of arrest and will support you if this comes to pass. A number of organizations have also intentionally had White activists use their bodies for protection of BIPOC activists by standing on the perimeter to serve as a barrier as BIPOC activists speak or act—police and counterprotestors are less likely to use violence against White activists than BIPOC activists.

You may also choose to engage in antiracism work that generally has lower levels of physical harm such as work around policy, advocacy, petitions, boycotts, journalism, and community programming. Even this work doesn't guarantee immunity from consequences—people who engage in these efforts have also faced threat and harm—but there may be a lesser overall degree of risk. Finally, you can also toggle between the two, working to find a balance between more drastic antiracist action and action that's more covert or strictly supportive. The cause of racial justice is important—and so is your life and safety.

Before we move on, a word about the effort among some BIPOC to assimilate into racist, capitalist society as a form of survival in it. As a BIPOC, you may have come to believe that the best form of resistance or survival is the accumulation of wealth for yourself and your family. You may fear that engaging in antiracism action will cost you and your family, financially and professionally. Or you may believe that education and wealth will be enough to protect you and your family from racism.

The reality is that antiracist activists have faced economic and professional costs. At the same time, it is also true that education and wealth have not been effective shields against the brutality of racism. BIPOC who have achieved high levels of success have shared stories of racial profiling, police brutality, discrimination in stores and neighborhoods, harassment in the workplace, and inequity in the quality of health care. It's true that finance and education open some doors, but they alone do not dismantle racism.

For your edification, please complete the exercise below. Consider the fact that education and wealth are usually beneficial at the individual level and/or to your immediate family. This may boost areas of your life while still leaving you, your loved ones, and the larger community facing racial stress and trauma. No amount of privilege from education and wealth leaves you entirely immune from racism. While education and wealth may position you to do important antiracism work and to empower those you support, it is important to not mistakenly believe that attaining those goals will automatically protect you or others from racism.

Things I Gain from Education	Things I Gain from Wealth	Things I Gain from Racial Justice

Take a moment to consider the chart you just completed. What do you gain and what do others gain by you achieving your goals in each category? We hope you'll remain clear in your commitments to antiracism as a specific goal, beyond degrees and wealth creation. We hope you'll look for ways to empower not only you and your family but the larger community and society, especially those who are systematically marginalized.

Another fear you may face as a BIPOC is the fear that justice for one race will block or diminish justice for your race/ethnicity. We have seen this happen: BIPOC fighting each other for crumbs while the majority of resources are still in the hands of White people.

These oppositions between BIPOC communities— created, reinforced, and highlighted by White supremacy—do in some cases stem from real tensions. Different groups have been given different positions in the racial hierarchy. And it's one of the functions of that hierarchy to drive the groups in it to infighting, over the privileges they are or aren't getting and over resources they believe are scarce, rather than permitting the solidarity that comes from knowing you're all part of the same system.

But these oppositions between BIPOC create barriers to solidarity work that can more effectively dismantle White supremacy. Historically, when coalitions have been made and maintained between BIPOC communities, powerful actions have been possible. What's more, committing to being antiracist is broader than solely wanting justice for your group. If you're antiracist, it means you want racial justice for everyone.

One way to shift this fear is to challenge the scarcity mindset, by dreaming a bigger dream, where there is room for everyone at the table. Dr. Winne Ng in 2012 noted that interracial movements help to counter division and fear by mobilizing antiracism education and political action.

Complete the table below to challenge your fears about racial empowerment and equity for groups other than your own. In the second row, we provide some hypothetical responses to give you an idea about ways you may think about completing the table.

I fear if other BIPOC groups get more, my group will suffer in the following ways:	This fear is based on the following experiences or observations:	I can shift my thoughts about the fear by considering:	When I shift my thinking, I notice this change in my emotions:	When I shift my thoughts and feelings, I am free to:	
Black people will have fewer businesses, jobs, housing, political opportunities if Latinx have more	Seeing the loss of Black communities, businesses, and political seats	There are enough resources in the US for both groups to have housing, jobs, and political power. Figuring out what this looks like will take ongoing honest reflection and conversations, and it's also possible.	Less tense, anxious, and fearful	Advocate for all BIPOCs rights and resources. Continue paying attention to the biases that might enter my thinking—and know to ascribe these to racist ideas I've been socialized to hold.	

BIPOC AND WHITE PEOPLE CONFRONTING FEAR OF INADEQUACY

No matter the racial group(s) of which you're a member, you may have fears of inadequacy. You may fear getting things wrong, saying the wrong thing, doing the wrong thing, or being imperfect. Let us assure you that you'll be imperfect. There is no such thing as a perfect person and no such thing as a perfect antiracist. Antiracism is a lifelong journey of learning and living and revising. You cannot let the fear of errors keep you stuck and stagnant.

Instead, we suggest approaching the work with openness, humility, and a commitment to survive and outlast the mistakes, missteps, and errors along the way, learning from those experiences rather than letting them stop you. We are all flawed and will miss things. The key is to have the courage to learn from the mistakes you make, to take ownership of those mistakes and apologize when needed, and try again. And the next time, you'll have more awareness and knowledge than you had before. Reject notions of perfectionism and inadequacy, which hinder you more than they help, by being patient with yourself, gracious with others, and setting an intention to grow from the past.

Learning and practicing the skills of self-soothing and self-regulation will be invaluable in this. Let's explore one such practice now.

Embodied Healing—Comfort Hold

There will be times when your fear of getting it wrong or saying it wrong will be overwhelming. While community support is vital, it is also important to learn how to soothe and regulate yourself. In 2020, Dr. Gail Parker, psychologist and yoga teacher, published the book *Restorative Yoga for Ethnic and Race-Based Stress and Trauma*, in which she notes the traumatic impact and emotional wounds of racism as well as the ways we can use stillness and movement to restore us. We want to introduce three postures for you to experiment with to see if any of them help you to breathe through the fear and settle your nervous system.

Hold 1: Sit on the floor with your legs crossed or in a chair with your feet on the ground. Cross your arms over your chest and allow them to reach your back. Remain in this hug position as you take five cleansing breaths.

Hold 2: Sit on the floor with your legs crossed or in a chair with your feet on the ground. Place one hand over your heart and one over your abdomen. Remain in this place of rest and calm for five cleansing breaths.

Hold 3: Lay on your side in the fetal position. Your arms may be in front of your chest, with one hand resting on your face. Remain in this place of rest for five minutes.

You may practice these holds now and also in moments when you're feeling anxious or afraid. Again, learning to tolerate any distress you might feel and to soothe yourself is an important strategy to keep in mind as you shift from developing an antiracist mindset to beginning an active antiracism practice.

Appropriate Responses to Constructive Correction

In addition to using your calming techniques, it is also important to take responsibility for any offense or harm created by errors made in antiracism action. Sometimes we get overwhelmed when we don't know what to do or we feel powerless, embarrassed, or defensive about mistakes we have made. Here is a quick formula for addressing microaggressions and other offenses in antiracism work:

1. Really listen. Sometimes we jump into being defensive or even to apologizing when we have not truly understood what happened or what we did that caused harm. Take a breath and set the aim of listening without simply planning your defense.

2. Really think through the actions or words that are the point of concern. Sometimes people who have said or done racist things, including microaggressions, demand that the harmed person overexplain the problem and/or take emotional care of the person who committed the offense. You want to be careful not to ask that the harmed person teach you in the moment or even immediate aftermath in which they are coping with the wound of the action. Additionally, you'll want to take care not to verbally or nonverbally express a sense of entitlement: for example, expecting an instant acceptance of your apology or to be comforted around your feelings of distress.

3. Once you have an understanding of what has happened, you'll want to offer an apology, without waiting for the person or other people to suggest that you apologize. The apology should be specific in naming the behavior that was wrong and acknowledging your awareness of the harm that it caused.

4. A sincere apology will not include a justification of the behavior or a blaming of the person you're apologizing to. For example, do not add statements such as: *I'm sorry you took it that way. I didn't realize you were sensitive. If I said anything that was hurtful (no acknowledgment or awareness), I'm sorry. I really need you to accept my apology. I hope you know no one is perfect.*

5. An authentic apology should be followed by changed behavior. If you apologize and continue doing the same behavior, the apology is not going to be experienced as sincere. The changed behavior may also include corrective action to address the harm that was done by the original action. For example, if you took credit for a BIPOC's work, you may send out an email to those involved acknowledging the work of the BIPOC person who was erased.

EXERCISE: A Trip Down Memory Lane

As you prepare to transition with us from adopting a mindset of being willing to confront racism to activation, where you actually engage in antiracism, let's complete one final exercise.

In the space below, reflect on one time you were successful in confronting your fears. Consider something you were afraid to do, but did anyway, which turned out well. When we remember the successes of our past, even if they were not in the realm of antiracism, it can give us confidence in our own ability to act and achieve and the courage to move forward despite our fears.

_____

_____

_____

_____

_____

_____

PART 3

Taking Action to Cultivate an Antiracist Life

We're glad you're staying on the journey with us and hope you've been able to think compassionately about your process. You have already invested time and energy in reflecting on the foundational concepts that are the basis for antiracism. Then, in Part 2, you explored a number of psychological roadblocks on the journey. Now we hope you're ready to begin, revitalize, or deepen your antiracism action. It's not enough to reflectively stand against racism in your mind and heart if this reflection never leads to concrete action.

In the next part, you'll discover a number of ways you can translate antiracist values into action. We'll show you some important steps toward integrating antiracism in your interpersonal relationships both within your family and friendship circles and in your public life. You'll also learn how to take antiracist action to shift institutions, communities, and larger society through policies and practices.

We then will share our perspective on topics we think too many people leave out of the conversation: bringing antiracism to your parenting (or mentoring) and to your spiritual or religious community. We want you to be empowered to not leave antiracism out of any aspect of your life. We invite you to take a cleansing breath, work at your own pace, and remember the goal of this book is not speed but actual application. Try not to stop at the point of reading but to actually practice beyond the page and integrate the activities in your life. Let's begin.

CHAPTER 8

Navigating People, Places, and Spaces from an Antiracist Perspective

We're excited that you're still on the journey with us as we shift from internal processes—understanding what racism is and addressing the barriers that can hinder antiracist work—to the external work that is needed to combat racism. In the previous section, we talked about facing barriers, shifting our perspective, and challenging our default ways of thinking, or liberating our minds so that we can more consistently engage in antiracism efforts. Some of the barriers we covered earlier in this handbook were ignorance, indifference, avoidance, and guilt. And to address these barriers, we encouraged you to educate yourself about race and racism as a way of taking responsibility as well as to confront stereotypes you might hold or encounter in others—slowly taking steps to shift your perspective to an antiracist one. We also discussed liberating your mind from indifference, avoidance, and guilt by fostering humility around what you know and what you don't know, and facing your fears about what might happen if you engage in antiracist action. A key aspect of your journey to educate yourselves and surmount these barriers was to become more aware of our country's living history of race and racism and the way in which power and privilege play out in your life and the lives of others. From this place of increased awareness, we want you to recognize those moments when you're called to not only shift your mindset but to also move into antiracist action.

We hope that you'll be able to build on all of the work you've done in the earlier part of the handbook in identifying and working through some of the psychological barriers to antiracist practice. Meanwhile, in this chapter, the focus moves to action. We will offer strategies to help you put antiracism into practice across various contexts: in the places and spaces where you spend the most time in your everyday life and with the people you encounter there. The *people* we might interact with when we take antiracist action include our family and friends, coworkers or bosses, or strangers we interact with in our community or in public settings. The *places* and *spaces* include our homes and neighborhoods, professional settings, and community and public settings. (Note that we'll be focusing on your immediate surroundings and circumstances for now; in the next chapter, we'll look at antiracism through community, civic, and political engagement.)

The unfortunate reality is that as long as we live in a society in which racism exists (reinforcing a racial hierarchy built on White supremacy), people will continue to confront racial discrimination. The impact of racism falls most frequently and directly on those of us who are Black, Indigenous, or people of color, and is experienced through any number of discriminatory racial encounters, or DREs (Anderson and Stevenson 2019). DREs can manifest across the multiple levels on which racism is expressed (e.g., individual, cultural, and systemic). You may also be familiar with the term *racial microaggressions*, which are a type of DRE and refer to everyday occurrences of racial discrimination that include insults and slights faced by those who are BIPOC (Sue and colleagues 2007).

The strategies you use to put antiracism into action will vary based on the type of discriminatory racial encounters you face or witness. We want to emphasize, as you contemplate the move from internal reflection to externally directed action, that the health and well-being of you and your community are of paramount importance. Maintaining commitment to antiracism requires emotional labor; there may also be concrete consequences for the antiracist actions you undertake, especially if you belong to a group disadvantaged by the racial hierarchy. Acknowledging these realities is key to being able to sustain your antiracist efforts. Decisions about when and where to engage in antiracism efforts should be grounded in your sense of how well the action reflects your values and beliefs about justice and equity, while also considering the social and emotional resources you're able to draw upon to promote health, well-being, and safety for you and your community. You'll also want to consider the potential pros and cons of the action you're contemplating at the particular point in time. Let's turn now to the strategies we recommend you use when it comes time to *act* as an antiracist in the world.

STRATEGIES FOR PUTTING ANTIRACISM INTO PRACTICE

When you're confronted with racism in an interpersonal interaction, there are several ways you can put the antiracism mindset you've been cultivating into practice.

1. Read the situation at hand: who is involved and what is going on?

2. Focus on how the encounter conflicts with the values you hold about antiracism.

3. Consider your options for how to respond. Assess the power dynamics at play in the situation and ask yourself: who holds power here?

4. Determine your ability to manage the situation as constructively as possible; how can you maintain integrity and enact your values?

5. Decide whether to take direct action or exit the situation (and perhaps do something later).

6. Take time to reflect on what happened.

We've said a lot here, so let's go through each of these steps and explore in more detail what's involved in each one.

Read the situation at hand: who is involved and what is going on in the interaction?

First things first: recognize that you're confronting racism. You'll then continue to assess the situation by focusing on who is involved and what behaviors are taking place. This process is a key part of the racial literacy skills we discussed with you earlier in the workbook. Stevenson (2014) describes the ability to read racially stressful encounters as interpreting and appraising the situation at hand, with an eye to the racial dynamics at play. Some factors you might want to consider as you read the situation include:

- Who is involved?

- Where are you (e.g., home, work, in public)?

- Is this a one-time occurrence or something that has happened over time in a relationship with another person?

Focus on how the encounter conflicts with the values you hold about antiracism.

Once you've read the situation, it's time to check in with yourself as to whether the values you hold about antiracism are being challenged by this particular interaction. Be clear about what your values are (justice, fairness, respect, and so on). Ask yourself which of these values is being violated in the situation you're facing. Identify how the encounter is at odds with those values—and in what ways? If someone makes a statement that is based in racist stereotypes, you must be clear about your beliefs that those statements are not true, cause harm to members of a particular racial group, and run counter to your values about truth, justice, and equity. This will help focus how you might respond to the encounter.

Consider your response options; assess the power dynamics.

Once you've clarified your values, begin to consider how you might respond. In the moments when you're encountering racism, it is important to be able to assess the power dynamics of the situation. You may remember from our earlier discussion of power (chapter 3) that we highlighted the different levels of power we might hold in a given situation, which included "power over" and "power to." We want you to be confident that you have the power within you to say or do something when you encounter racism.

However, it's also necessary to be aware of the power dynamics in a given situation and to realistically assess the extent to which you and whoever you're interacting with have the power to exert influence—and what type of influence—in that moment. This is one of the points that psychologist Derald Wing Sue, a leading scholar on racism and racial microaggressions, and his colleagues (2019) emphasize in their work on "microintervention" strategies—or the direct, problem-focused actions that validate and affirm the targets of racial microaggressions.

You must consider power differentials that exist between perpetrators and targets when you're deciding what action to take. You'll need to be aware of whether you're a target or bystander in the interaction, and what power dynamics exist with the other person(s) who are part of the interaction (e.g., family elder, police officer, etc.).

Determine your ability to manage the situation as constructively as possible.

Choose your response strategy based on what approach will allow you to maintain your sense of integrity and live out your antiracist values. The reality is that, due to power dynamics related to the racial hierarchy, you must be clear about the extent to which those you're interacting with have the power to harm you or others, or compromise your safety or security in some way. Your sense of integrity as someone who believes in racial justice and equality should be considered, alongside what may happen if you do take action *and* what harm could be done if you don't take action. For example, choosing to film someone being harassed by the police might provide another layer of accountability to help bring about racial justice, and in that way, elevate you to be more of an active participant or bystander in the situation. Moreover, you might even save a life.

Decide whether to take direct action or exit the situation.

Decide if you'll confront the situation directly in the moment or exit the situation. If you choose the latter, you can follow up at a later time, if possible or desired, or let the situation pass. Direct action may involve trying to defuse the situation or educating another person by making them aware of how their behavior is problematic. If you choose to take direct action, we believe it is important that you name the problem behavior and describe why it's problematic. It may be that the other person is not willing or able to accept your response, though in some ways, that's to be expected. Just as it's not your responsibility when a perpetrator of racism behaves in the way that they do, you're not responsible for whether they acknowledge or change their behavior. You may want to consider at what point you'll end the interaction after you've responded.

The stakes are obviously going to be different when the person you're interacting with is someone you have an ongoing relationship with such as a friend, family member, or colleague. In this case, you're not just deciding whether to take direct action or exit a conversation or situation limited to that time or space; you may also be considering whether you need to adjust or exit a relationship. You may decide to make a clear statement that what just happened was unacceptable to you and you no longer want to continue interacting with the offending person right now. In this case, you may follow up with the person or other people who were present during the situation at a later time.

Take time to reflect on what happened.

Once the encounter has ended, ask yourself how you felt during the encounter and make a note of it. Then consider: are you able to access a support system to help you process your feelings? Remember, antiracist action is emotional labor, and we want you to identify and make use of a network that will provide you the social and emotional support you need. You might also consider what lessons you might take away from this encounter that will make the next antiracist action easier.

What About More Proactive Approaches to Putting Antiracism into Practice?

The above strategies are for you to use when you confront racially discriminatory encounters that are unexpected (in that you didn't plan for them to occur). But what about when you want to lead efforts to address the racism that you've seen play out in spaces such as the workplace? How might you use the strategies we reviewed above to be a proactive agent of change?

In this situation, your first step is observing how racism has manifested, interpersonally, culturally, or structurally. This aligns with *reading the situation*: who is involved and what is going on. You would then focus on how the racism (whether interpersonally, culturally, or structurally) *conflicts with your values*. While you've already made the decision to engage in antiracist action in order to be an agent of change, being clear about the power dynamics at play will inform your strategy and how you can manage the situation as constructively as possible. After taking action, we still recommend taking time to *reflect on what happened* and continuing to engage your support network so that you can continue your antiracist practice.

In addition to applying our model to pro-active antiracism, we want to provide some additional strategies for bringing antiracism to your social network: (1) encourage others to read this and other resources on antiracism; (2) start a book or film club focused on anti-racism; (3) diversify your friendship circle to build personal relationships with people outside of your race; (4) talk with friends and family about racial justice issues to raise awareness; and (5) proactively promote ideals of racial justice and inclusion among your family members, friends, and co-workers.

EXERCISE: Reflections on Putting Antiracism Strategies into Practice

Now we want you to take some time to reflect on the strategies we laid out for you and apply them to a set of scenarios that represent a range of discriminatory racial encounters. Use the space below to respond to one or more of the following scenarios in which you've previously been, or anticipate that you might be, faced with a discriminatory racial encounter:

• A family member or friend uses a racial slur or tells a racist joke in your presence.

• For BIPOC: a family member or friend makes a derogatory remark about another member of a BIPOC community that reflects colorism and/or anti-Blackness.

• You are racially profiled in a store (or witness someone else being profiled in this way).

• For BIPOC: during a staff meeting, you're asked to represent the "_____" experience.

• You work at an organization where the leadership team is all White and BIPOC employees consistently receive more negative evaluations and do not get the same opportunities for advancement as their White counterparts.

Read the situation at hand: who is involved and what is going on in the interaction?

_____

_____

_____

Focus on how the encounter conflicts with the values you hold about antiracism.

_____

_____

_____

Consider your response options; assess the power dynamics.

_____

_____

_____

Determine your ability to manage the situation as constructively as possible.

_____

_____

_____

Decide whether to take direct action or exit the situation. Or what direct action you plan to take to proactively address racism.

_____

_____

_____

Take time to reflect on what happened.

_____

_____

_____

After you've completed this exercise, here's some additional food for thought: First, there are costs to silence and inaction, both for the self and others. Acknowledge those costs as you make decisions.

Second, you should expect to feel discomfort when you're challenging people on their biases and problematic behavior, especially when it comes to race and racism, given the fraught ways that we have been socialized to think about and address (or not) race and racism as well as how we experience the emotional impact of being advantaged or disadvantaged by race and racism. Don't let discomfort stop you from taking action. Know that there will be growing pains as you choose to engage in antiracist action more frequently. You'll also get more comfortable and confident the more you take action.

Third, as you sustain your antiracist engagement, continue to reflect on and reassess what worked well for you within specific situations. Identify what you want to continue to do and what you might do differently in a future circumstance.

Finally, resist the idea of a hierarchy of antiracism strategies, in which direct action is viewed as more valuable or impactful than indirect action—for example, attending a protest as opposed to writing a letter to a city councilperson to establish your support for an antiracist cause. Different approaches can and will work for different people in different situations. And we need a range of strategies, taken as a whole, to help bring about change. What's more, the most effective strategy for you in any given moment will be the one that best aligns with your personality, in the tone and style that are most natural to you. You'll want to push yourself to take risks and grow, but also to be as authentic as you can in this process and to make sure your antiracism is sustainable for you.

A quick note here for our White readers. As you worked through one or more of the scenarios above, you may have had to ask yourself what it would mean for you to confront discriminatory racial encounters as a bystander or perpetrator (or think back to past experiences in this role). As we've discussed, power and privilege accompany Whiteness in our society. We want to encourage you to grow your antiracist practice so that you're an authentic ally, advocate, or co-conspirator (or someone who, as Alicia Garza describes, not only talks the talk but shows up and acts in solidarity) with BIPOC.

EXERCISE: Your Antiracist Role Mode

Identify someone of your racial group who has stood up to racism. This person can be a well-known current or historical figure and/or someone you personally know. Use the space below to describe: 1) what you admire about this person, and 2) what you would like to apply from this person's example to your antiracist journey.

_____

_____

_____

_____

_____

_____

   Read what you've written above and think about what type of example you'll be setting for others as you continue to cultivate your own antiracist engagement. And keep this imagined ideal in mind going forward. We'll explore in the next chapter how you can extend your antiracist efforts from interpersonal interactions to advocacy of antiracist policies and practices.

CHAPTER 9

Changing Our Communities through Antiracist Practices and Policies

At the outset of our work together here, we stressed that each of us—BIPOC and White—learns about race and racism in both overt and implicit ways as we grow and develop into the unique people we are. As we make the commitment to antiracist action, we all need to grapple with and better understand our living history of race and racism while we address the psychological barriers that keep us from being antiracist.

In our previous chapter, we spent time exploring how each of us can take steps to put antiracism into action in interpersonal interactions we have with family, friends, and colleagues, or in public settings with those we don't know personally. And while our personal growth and interpersonal interactions are important in our commitment to antiracism, we also know that individual work is not sufficient since we exist not in isolation but as members of families, friendship circles, and communities. We all participate in workplaces, neighborhoods, schools, places of worship, and other civic institutions—each of which can be a place where racism persists and is reinforced.

You'll remember from earlier in the handbook (see chapter 1) that racism is not just about individual beliefs or behavior; it operates at and across multiple levels: individual, internalized, cultural, and institutional/structural (or systemic) levels. In this chapter, we're going to take a closer look at the latter two levels—the cultural and the systemic.

The racism we might experience in our communities is the cultural and systemic expressions of racism that in turn shapes the *policies and practices* that set the context for all of our lives—where we live or go to school, how we can wear our hair when we go to work, whether our families have accumulated wealth over time, or how healthy we or our families are. We have seen this play out in stark reality over the course of the recent pandemic in terms of who was more likely to contract COVID-19 and eventually die from it.

Addressing systems, structures, and institutions is necessary if we want to extend our antiracist efforts beyond individual interactions toward a more collective impact (Smedley 2019). This requires an awareness of the systemic ways that policy and practice have served to reproduce racial inequality. Increasing this awareness can prevent us from deficit-thinking, where we view individual members of racially disadvantaged communities as the problem or inherently lacking in some way when it is often racially unjust policies and practices across systems and structures that serve to block the health and progress of members of those communities (Fine and Cross 2016). We can also take a closer look at the practices and policies that shape our broader communities, determining how they might reinforce racism and inequity, and how we might be able to change them. In this chapter, we'll guide you through steps toward antiracist engagement that can help transform practices and policies and move us closer to racial equity.

PRACTICES, POLICIES, AND TARGETS FOR ACTION

Let's explore what we mean by "practices" and "policies." Practices are the tactics we use to carry out certain activities or programs at work, in our communities, in civic spaces, or within systems. "Practice" can also refer to professional actions, for those of us who work in service to others—for example, in professions that focus on health and healing. Policies consist of rules, laws, and regulations that address how our society functions across the systems that shape people's lives such as education, health care, and laws. Both formal and informal policies shape our practices. And more broadly, we can think of social or public policy as policies crafted and enforced by government or larger institutions to address the most relevant issues and problems we face in our society (Maton et al., 2017).

So how can we shift our policies and practices to be antiracist? What do we actually *do* to change policies or practices that will bring about racial equity in our civic and community spaces? Recently, Camara Jones (2020), a physician and epidemiologist who has studied racism and health for decades, described two types of targets for antiracist action that may be helpful here. One target is to address structural aspects of our society like residential segregation based on race or disproportionate incarceration rates for Black and Brown communities: these are *structural targets* for antiracist action. The second are *values targets*: the social and cultural beliefs people hold that serve as barriers to racial equity at the cultural and systemic level. Examples of values targets for antiracism action include: challenging beliefs that focus on the individual at the expense of acknowledging our interdependence, which can block the potential for collective action and impact; ahistorical perspectives that limit our understanding of the impact of racism over time and the possibilities to challenge it; and myths such as meritocracy (which blames individuals and communities for the disadvantages they face) and zero-sum thinking (or the belief that if some people gain something then other people must lose).

There are any number of structural and values targets for antiracism action where you can focus your attention. To help illustrate the process of addressing both structural and values targets for antiracist action in an organizational setting, we'll share here the experience of working with BIPOC faculty and staff at predominantly White schools that wanted to promote the success of BIPOC students on-campus.

Case Study: Experiences of BIPOC Students and Faculty/ Administration in Predominantly White Schools

You may be aware of the recent social media campaign that explored the experiences of Black students at predominantly White, elite independent, and suburban schools. Students used the "Black@" (or "Black at") hashtag to describe their experiences with racial microaggressions and discrimination in their school settings. "Black@" resonated with us since one of the authors has been involved in research and consultation focused on the success of Black students in their schools— particularly schools where they are in the racial minority. Through this work, we heard concerns from students, families, and administrators about discriminatory experiences students encountered, there not being enough BIPOC students enrolled in these schools, and BIPOC students leaving the school more often than their White counterparts. Similar dynamics were noted for BIPOC faculty and administrators. To better ground our antiracism work in the schools, we looked at both the structures and values shaping student, family, and faculty/administrator experiences.

We thought it was important to know and explore several questions about the circumstances of students' lives, both inside and outside the schools. Which families are more likely to have money to pay tuition to attend elite independent schools? How are residential patterns shaped by race and income? And how might these patterns relate to the resources that are available to local public schools in urban and suburban areas? When these schools are hiring, how does access to the elite colleges and universities that independent schools often recruit from influence the diversity of faculty and administrators that are hired? And how does the diversity of the work environment relate to faculty experiences of belonging, experiences of racism at work, and the likelihood of retention?

We also wanted to explore the values that shaped school dynamics and student, family, and faculty experiences. This included exploring perceptions about Black students and families that were grounded in ahistorical views on racism, especially as they relate to the myth of meritocracy. In school environments where these myths go unchallenged, assumptions are often made about students' abilities and capacity for achievement. For instance, certain students are assumed to be more capable than others. At the same time, students who are facing challenges in school are told that they just need to study more or change their behavior in some way to better fit in while the impact that racism and race-related stress may be having on their achievement and sense of belonging is downplayed, if acknowledged at all.

We wanted to hear from members of the school community about how their schools could be more welcoming and inclusive for all students. To that end, we engaged in interviews, focus groups, and surveys of students, families, and faculty/staff, and asked direct questions about race and racism. From here, we developed broad recommendations that were based on schools' unique contexts. They included encouraging schools to examine their policies around admissions and hiring, with a critical eye toward the structural barriers they may have been reinforcing with "business as usual." For instance, what assumptions are made about which candidates are the best fit for a school if the hiring committee limits their search to certain colleges or universities? We recommended schools expand their hiring pools as they reflected on what it means to really be inclusive in practice. We also suggested that schools develop practices (such as creating affinity groups for BIPOC students) that will promote a sense of belonging for students so that there are opportunities for them to be affirmed in their racial identity and places they can speak up if they encounter racism at school.

We hope hearing about the case study helped to illustrate how important it is to examine the structures and values that exist in community settings, organizations, or larger systems when you're considering antiracist action to change policies and practices in institutional and cultural contexts. Have any targets for your own work come to mind as you read the case study? We know that it may seem overwhelming to attempt to effect change at community, organizational, or institutional levels. You might not know where to start, or you might wonder if what you do will have an impact. We believe you can make a difference in your community, in the organizations you're a part of, and within systems as well. And we encourage you to take action. Following are some ways to get started.

Steps for Taking Antiracist Action in Communities, Organizations, and Systems

- Reflect on your spheres of influence.

- Identify the practices and policies in these spaces that reinforce racism and inequity.

- Determine what a first step to make change in your community, organizations, and within systems might look like (or a next step, if you're already engaged in the work).

- Find partners with whom you can work to take this step and make collective impact.

- Sustain your efforts by building your support systems and putting strategies in place that will help ensure progress continues.

In the next exercise, we'll work on these steps so you can get a better sense of how you can start to shift some of the practices and policies embedded in your spheres of influence and begin to bring about antiracist change.

EXERCISE: Your Spheres of Influence and Antiracist Practices and Policies

First, let's consider the places and spaces that shape your everyday life. Think back to the exercise you completed in chapter 2, where we asked you to identify your spheres of influence—those places where you're most able to make an impact such as your family, your place of work, where you worship, or in an online community. Select one of those spheres of influence and put it in the chart below.

Next, identify practices and policies in that sphere that might reinforce racism and inequality. Then determine what a first (or next) step in making systemic change might look like and consider which partners in your spheres of influence might be able to join you in the antiracist action you plan to take and work with you to make a collective impact. Finally, think about how you can sustain your efforts by getting support from others.

We'll use our case study from earlier in the chapter as an example to guide you through the exercise. Let's imagine that you're a faculty member at a suburban high school, making your workplace your sphere of influence. You notice that the BIPOC students at your school are in the racial minority, yet are disproportionately identified for more school disciplinary action than their White peers. You reach out to a longtime colleague to discuss your concerns and figure out where you could start to try and change things, and ultimately decide to convene a faculty committee to examine the extent to which faculty and administration are relying on practices that lead to racial inequity in how your school's policies impact students. You ask your colleague to chair the committee with you and also look to see which other faculty may want to join you in your efforts.

We've used this example to get you started in the exercise below. Now it's your turn to reflect on one of your spheres of influence and how you might begin to shift policies and practices toward antiracism. We've provided space for you to discuss more than one sphere of influence if you'd like to.

Sphere of Influence	Practices and Policies that Reinforce Racism	First (Or Next) Step to Making Change	Potential Partner for Collective Impact
The suburban high school where I am a faculty member	School disciplinary practices and policies	Convene a faculty committee to explore practices and policies	Longtime colleague to co-chair committee

We know it may be overwhelming to think about how to change policies and practices, and hope that by breaking the process down to a few initial steps, the task will seem more manageable for you. But as a reminder, none of us exists in isolation, and trying to do this work alone can be difficult—especially when you move your focus to spheres of influence at the community, organizational, or systems level. Collaboration is the key to bringing about collective impact. This is especially true when we think about addressing institutional or systemic racism.

Clinical community psychologist Derek Griffith and his colleagues in psychology and public health (2007) speak to the importance of collaboration when they describe the role that antiracist community organizing can play in bringing about change. In their discussion of community health interventions to dismantle racism, Griffith and colleagues highlight the need for a Change Team—a diverse group of leaders within communities and organizations that work together to create and implement change efforts.

As your work for racial equity and justice develops, it will be important for you to join or create a group similar to a Change Team so that you receive the support you need and so that your antiracist action reflects the community you're working with and is relevant and empowering for them.

YOUR OPPORTUNITY TO BE AN ANTIRACIST CHANGE AGENT

We want you to take some time now to identify opportunities where you can be the change you wish to see in the systems that shape your communities and organizations. Think about systems that are of most interest to you because of the impact they have on your family or community—perhaps one of the systems we've spoken about in this chapter, like education, health care, and law, or another system. Your actions might involve taking the initiative to lead efforts at your job to advocate for changing your workplace policies so that they more directly address antiracism (for example, in hiring or procuring diverse vendors). They may include joining local campaigns for justice for an antiracist cause—such as the unlawful detainment of undocumented people. Or you may choose to participate in the political campaigns of antiracist candidates at the local, state, or national level. You may work to mobilize voters or even decide to run for office yourself. Think of the Black Lives Matter activists who were key to the antiracist community organizing we saw across the country over the last few years and who are now holding political office. Their journeys can be a source of inspiration for you.

EXERCISE: Stepping into Leadership in Your Communities and Organizations

Let's use the final exercise of the chapter to explore opportunities for you to take antiracist action and step into leadership at the community or organizational level. Think about a system(s) that most interests you: education, health care, law, politics, or some other context.

Next, use the space below to reflect on whether you are: *waiting* to get involved in taking antiracist action to making change in the system, ready to *join* efforts to take antiracist action in the system, or willing to make an investment in *leading* initiatives to accomplish antiracism.

If you're waiting, share what you're waiting for to become involved. If you're ready, which efforts, movements, and organizations would you like to be part of and why? Where might you be willing to make the investment to offer yourself for leadership to accomplish antiracism initiatives? What would that look like? For the *joining* and *leading* areas, describe the practices and policies where you see yourself focusing your attention, and what, to the best of your knowledge, you imagine yourself doing.

_____

_____

_____

_____

_____

_____

Now, before you proceed to make good on the goals you're writing down, we want to remind you of our discussion in an earlier chapter of this handbook about humility. Whether you're considering joining or stepping into leadership, remember to do so with humility. You have as much to learn from other people in leadership as they have to learn from you. Your efforts to take antiracist action will benefit from being grounded in humility, as will the communities and organizations with which you're working.

MINDFUL MOMENT: Sustainability

Antiracist commitment is a long-term, lifelong journey. Your efforts may ebb and flow at times, but the goal is to stay committed, knowing that one march or one vote does not end the journey. Review the exercises you completed throughout this chapter and think about how you'll feel when you know you've made an impact. Hopeful? Proud? Eager to do more? Hold on to these feelings; it takes time, energy, and resources to maintain your commitment to antiracist action. We will explore sustainability more in the final chapter of the handbook.

CHAPTER 10

Antiracism Parenting: Cultivating Courage and a Love for Justice

If we turned the clock back and told our parents that their young children would one day write an antiracism handbook, we can say with confidence that they wouldn't be surprised. Our parents were intentional about raising us with knowledge of not only who we are as African Americans but also the reality of racism and the necessity of actively resisting it. (While we have utilized the term "Black Americans" throughout the text to be inclusive of African immigrant Americans and Caribbean Americans, the two authors are African American specifically; we are descendants of enslaved Africans who were brought to the United States through the Trans-Atlantic Slave Trade.) The role that parents and other caretakers have in shaping the minds and lives of children is powerful and long-lasting.

Before we think about the role you can play in cultivating antiracism in the children in your life, let's take a moment to reflect on the impact your parents or caregivers had on your understanding of racism. We want you to consider what your parents taught you, either directly with words or indirectly by their actions. The messages you received may have promoted racism and indifference, or may have planted the seeds of your antiracist values today.

Let's consider some examples of verbal messages promoting either antiracism, or the idea that racism is wrong:

1.   Parents watching the reporting of a racially motivated hate crime on the evening news who turn to you and say, "That's racist. That is not right."

2. Parent saying to you as a child, "Never look down on someone or talk hatefully to someone just because they are a different race than you."

3. Parent telling you when an election was coming up, "I'm not voting for that person because they're racist. I don't support that."

On the other hand, examples of verbal messages that promote racism are:

1. "Black/Latinx/Asian/Native American people are always complaining and wanting a handout. They need to work hard like the rest of us."

2. "Affirmative action and calling everything racist is just reverse racism."

3. "White people are the real victims in this country. No one will speak up for us because they want to be politically correct. Meanwhile, minorities are taking everything."

As we noted earlier, antiracism messages are not just verbal in nature. Here are a few examples of nonverbal messages you may have received from parents/guardians regarding racism being unacceptable:

1. Watching your parents participate in antiracism organizations or protests.

2. Watching your parents engage respectfully with people of diverse races.

3. Watching your parents speak up when they witness or experience racism, or noticing that they no longer go to a store where they witnessed or experienced racism.

Nonverbal messages that you may have observed that supported racism include:

1. Seeing your parents get tense or angry in the presence of racially marginalized people, even people who were your friends or romantic partners.

2. Observing your parents being quick to grab their purse, get out of an elevator, or call the police when in the presence of racially marginalized people.

3. Witnessing your parents vote for, support, campaign for, and/or defend politicians who endorse racist views.

Let's use this next exercise to reflect on your personal experience. Please reflect honestly in the chart below by considering what your parents taught you about antiracist values and beliefs:

Antiracism Values/Beliefs	Verbal Message from Parents/Guardians	Nonverbal Message from Parents/Guardians
Racism is wrong, unfair, and unjust.		
Racism is pervasive.		
We need to promote fairness and justice.		
We have a responsibility to interrupt and work against racism.		
We have the power to make a difference in creating a more racially just world.		
Saying racist things is unacceptable in this family.		
Mistreating people of other races is unacceptable in this family.		
We can take initiative and lead antiracism efforts.		

As you reflect on the chart you completed above, take a moment to consider the verbal and nonverbal messages that you want to pass down to the children in your life. Please note that although we are using the term "parenting," we want to be inclusive of the multiple roles one may have in the life of a child: extended family member (aunt, grandparent, etc.), mentor, teacher, role model, family friend, or godparent.

Please journal below about how the way your parents demonstrated (or didn't demonstrate) antiracism is similar or different from the ways you want to parent or mentor (or already have) the children in your life. Build on your reflections from chapter 1 of the handbook, about the concepts of race and racism.

_____

_____

_____

_____

_____

_____

THE WHAT AND WHY OF ANTIRACISM PARENTING

You may be wondering, "What is antiracism parenting?" Great question. Antiracism parenting, in alignment with antiracism in general, is more than raising children who are aware that racism exists and is wrong. Antiracism parenting is intentionally raising children who have the commitment, courage, knowledge, and skills to combat racism and work toward racial justice. Racism does not wait until people are adults to reveal itself; likewise, antiracism is not only for adults either. Children and adolescents can be empowered with the awareness that they can make a difference in creating more justice in the world.

You may want to address antiracism with your children, but not know where to start. Let's address some of the cognitive and emotional hesitation that could keep you from discussing and modeling antiracism with your children. In the chart below, we list some arguments against raising antiracist children and the feelings that may be associated with those thoughts. In the last column, please provide a counterargument that makes a case for proactively engaging children in antiracist thinking and action.

Thought	Associated Feeling	Counterargument
Children should be able to have an innocent life without being bombarded with messages about negative things like racism.	Protective	
I don't want my children to be rejected for speaking up about racism.	Fear	
Telling my children about racism will make them afraid.	Anxiety	
Telling my BIPOC children about racism will make them insecure.	Protective	

Thank you for considering the benefits of antiracism parenting. In case you had difficulty coming up with counterarguments for the above statements, let's consider a few arguments for intentional antiracism parenting.

1. While children should live in a world free from racism, they do not. Racism is present and prevalent. Ignoring it leaves children unprepared and uninformed, whereas awareness and empowerment can give them emotional protection. (You can read more about this in psychologist Beverly Daniel Tatum's classic book *Why Are All the Black Kids Sitting Together in the Cafeteria?*)

2. There are times when speaking up against racism comes with consequences. People who want to promote or protect racism and racist behaviors may respond with anger, frustration, or rejection. As parents, we need to decide if we want to raise children who are unwilling to inconvenience themselves when others are suffering. Let us also consider the guilt and shame of those children who do and say nothing in the face of racism (when they realize it is wrong).

3. The gift of antiracism parenting is you're not only telling children about the horrors and terrors of racism but you're also equipping them to know they can make a difference. You're enhancing their sense of agency and voice.

4. Research shows that BIPOC children who experience positive racial/cultural socialization enjoy greater positive ethnic identity, fewer externalizing behaviors, lower fighting frequency, higher self-esteem, fewer internalizing problems, and better cognitive outcomes (psychologist Diane Hughes and colleagues in 2006).

5. Research also demonstrates that, as early as preschool, children notice racial differences and make valuations based on those differences that reflect the racial hierarchy. It's up to parents and other influences to shape what kids think and feel about those differences. Silence will lead them to adopt the prevalent views in society, which are soaked in racism.

STRATEGIES FOR RAISING ANTIRACIST CHILDREN

While we could write a whole book on this topic (and possibly will!), we want to share three key strategies for raising antiracist children: *consciousness-raising*, *bystander intervention training*, and *pro-social antiracism engagement*. These strategies are based in liberation psychology, which originated in Latin America and teaches that racism is harmful and that a part of healing is empowerment to resist racism and other forms of oppression. Lillian Comas-Díaz and Edil Torres Rivera have written about liberation psychology in their groundbreaking 2020 book *Liberation Psychology: Theory, Method, Practice, and Social Justice*. In it, they discuss consciousness-raising, empowerment, and social justice action as tools for emancipation and to enhance well-being holistically. An additional resource that you may find helpful is *How to Talk So Kids Can Learn About Antiracism and Social Justice* by Nicola Davies, also published in 2020.

Consciousness-Raising

To raise antiracist children, you'll need to teach your children to have racial literacy. As we shared in the first chapter of this handbook, a key part of racial literacy is the ability to read racially stressful events and to understand the diverse ways that racism may manifest. Without racial literacy, people are limited in their ability to see racism and therefore do not respond to it. People who are hesitant to acknowledge racism will never conclude that they need to do something about it.

Raising children's consciousness around racism requires teaching them, in age-appropriate ways, a more complete and accurate history of racism in the United States. When we say "age-appropriate," what does that mean? Well, for example, we might let elementary-aged children know that some people have been harmed and mistreated because of racism, but we would not promote showing young children graphic pictures of the torture that people of color have endured. We could also share about the courageous ways that victims of racism and their allies have spoken up and resisted these harms, and teach about the diverse ways that racism shows up in our society and children's lives. This might include teaching children about name-calling or making jokes about racially marginalized people, who is left out of social gatherings, who faces unfair treatment in the media, justice system, and education system, and who gets access to quality health care and safety. When you're mindful of racism and can point it out to children, they will develop the skills to notice it themselves even when you're not present and will be aware that this is not fair. They can come back and tell you about what they noticed. In the next part, we will share some ideas around different things kids can do about racism.

It's important to pay attention to the developmental stage and unique personality of each child. Let's practice some developmentally appropriate ways to begin or continue raising your child's consciousness about racism in the exercise below.

EXERCISE: Brainstorming Antiracism Parenting

Use the chart below to consider how you might explain each form of racism to children, depending on their developmental stage. We recognize that each child is unique, so after you brainstorm about children in general, the last column is for you to think about how you would feel comfortable specifically educating your child. The approach you take with your child may match one of the earlier columns you completed, or it may be a new idea that aligns with your child's interests and personality. For example, if your child feels things deeply and is artistic, you may want to use the arts to raise awareness and perhaps focus more on solutions than on the pain of oppression.

Manifestations of Racism	Elementary-aged Children	Neurodiverse Children	Adolescents	Ways You Would Feel Comfortable Speaking to Your Specific Child(ren)
Racially motivated name-calling, teasing				
Racism in their education (lack of diversity in schoolbooks, encounters in the school setting, etc.)				
Racism in the criminal justice system (policing, etc.)				
Racism and poverty (homelessness, job opportunities, Internet access, etc.)				

While the above examples are about racism in the larger world, including the school environment, we want to acknowledge that there may be intergenerational conflict, in which your parents or other extended family members may promote racist ideas and behaviors that you do not support.

If that is the case, we invite you to reflect below about what you want to say to your children about the racist things that they may hear or witness from elders or others in your family. Additionally, what if anything will you say or do directly to address the family member who is promoting racism in the presence of your child(ren)? While this is challenging because of the discomfort that confrontation may cause, it is important to note that antiracism cannot be limited to your public life. Your values and commitment need to also show up in your private/personal life, including the ways you interact with your family.

_____

_____

_____

_____

_____

As you advance in your antiracist parenting, you'll want to be sure to bring to your children's attention the concept of intersectionality (not necessarily using that word, depending on their age and development). Help your children to notice the differences in treatment for people who are racially marginalized and also have a disability, are a religious minority, are LGBTQ+, are gender-diverse, are immigrants, etc. If this feels overwhelming, consider it an opportunity to expose your children to the rich diversity of lived experiences that people have.

Bystander Training

Once you teach children to notice racism, you can begin to actively and directly teach them how to intervene and interrupt when they see racism happening. BIPOC youth may be in the car with a friend or family member who is racially profiled and harassed by police. They may be in a classroom where a teacher makes a racist comment about their community. They may notice racial differences in how guidance counselors or school security officers respond to other BIPOC youth versus White youth.

White children may see children or even a teacher mistreating another child who is racially marginalized. As a teen, they may be at the mall with a friend and see that friend being followed, disrespected, and racially profiled by a store clerk. They may be at a family gathering and hear a relative make a racist remark.

These important moments require courage, safety, and strategies to intervene. The section Strategies for Putting Antiracism into Practice that we outlined in chapter 8 can be introduced to your child as you also consider the pointers below.

Bystander training involves centering the victim, so it is important to check in with the person being harmed (if that person is present). Centering the victim can look like making eye contact with the person, going to stand next to them, asking them if they are okay in the moment or after, or asking them if they would like you to walk with them.

When it comes to addressing the offender, your child can consider a number of strategies. (As you think about teaching your children these strategies, consider the age of your child, their temperament, how well they can assess the safety of the situation, and the different responses you may want to encourage, depending on the age of the person committing the racist act.)

One strategy is making eye contact with the offender and communicating with your facial expression that you don't like what is being said or done. Another is to say any of the following, depending on the child's relationship with the person and your child's personal safety:

1. I disagree.

2. That's a harmful/mean thing to say.

3. I don't like hearing you say mean things about other races or about my friend, etc.

4. I feel sad/upset when I hear you say that.

5. I didn't know you thought like that.

6. Stop.

The child/youth can also ask for clarification. Sometimes when we ask people to repeat the racist thought, they will hear themselves and try to amend their statement. This can be especially powerful when the request for clarification is coming from a child. (Of course, some people will stand by their statement and repeat it boldly.) The child can say:

1. I don't think I understood that. Can you say that again?

2. Are you really saying you believe…? (repeating back what the other person said)

Some people have also found it helpful to change the subject or use humor to defuse the tension of the moment. It's also important for your child to know that even if they don't interrupt racism in the moment, they can report what they observed to you or other adults. Let them know that you'll do what is in your power to address the situation(s): for example, filing a complaint at the store or meeting with the teacher. Whatever action you take, be sure to tell your child, so they are empowered to know that you'll support them in whatever ways you can.

EXERCISE: Personal Challenge

Make a commitment to having a conversation with your child in the next day or two about bystander intervention and taking action when they see racism. After you've had the conversation, reflect below on:

1) how you felt before having the conversation

_____

_____

_____

2) how your child responded

_____

_____

_____

3) how you're feeling now about the conversation

_____

_____

_____

Prosocial Antiracism Engagement

Prosocial actions are taken based on compassion for others, as opposed to in service of one's self. It's important to note that for BIPOC children in particular, antiracism work is in service of themselves *and* others. Antiracism work is not merely responding to individual slights, discrimination, and offenses in the moment. It's also about being proactively involved in work that promotes racial justice and liberation.

Some antiracism engagement that your child could become involved in includes:

1. Joining a racial affinity group or group for allies at their school or in the community: school clubs, rites of passage programs that teach BIPOC children about their culture and ways to resist racism, and youth subdivisions of racial justice community groups.

2. Starting and signing petitions that promote racial justice.

3. For those on social media, posting about racial justice—noting not only their beliefs or values but also raising awareness among their friends about racism and resources to combat it.

4. Participating in student government and making antiracism one of the student group's initiatives or priorities.

5. When picking topics for oral reports or art projects, selecting an antiracist topic. Your child can draw a picture, choreograph a dance, or write a poem about antiracism and racial justice. (There are even books like *Antiracism Starts with Me! A Coloring Book for Kids* by Kadeesha Bryant.)

6. Participating in antiracism marches and protests.

7. Adolescents can attend neighborhood or city council meetings and, during the time for public comment, consider giving a short statement about the importance of antiracism.

8. Raising money from family and friends to donate to an antiracism organization or to give to children who have lost a loved one as a result of a racially motivated hate crime.

CASE STUDY: PROFILE IN YOUTH ANTIRACISM ENGAGEMENT

The daughter of one of the authors, who is the goddaughter of the other author, has been engaged in prosocial antiracism engagement over the course of her fifteen years of life. As a young child, her family lived in a predominantly Latinx neighborhood and she attended a predominantly Jewish school. Her parents encouraged her to celebrate her heritage and learn ways to recognize and speak up about racism. As a result, she attended an annual summer camp for Black children to learn about Black culture, history, and arts. Along with her family, she attended a predominantly Black church, where sermons frequently addressed justice and empowerment. She participated in a Black History Month oratorical contest, to learn to use and celebrate her voice, and was subsequently the youngest speaker at a Black Lives Matter march, where she read a poem she wrote. As a high school student, she joined the Black Student Union and has advocated for the group to take actions to promote antiracism.

These engagements have not shielded her from the sting of racism, but through the support and preparation of her family, godmother, friends, and antiracism community, she is empowered to know that she can make a difference in the fight for racial justice.

EXERCISE: Fostering Antiracism for Your Children

Look at the list of potential actions provided above, consider your child's age and interests, and then share with them some possible ways they can become antiracist not only in how they think about others but also in action. In the space below, write about your experience talking with or taking steps to engage your child with antiracism:

_____

_____

_____

_____

_____

_____

_____

MINDFUL MOMENT: Conclusion

It can be beautiful and empowering to hold antiracism not only as an individual value but also as a family value that you pass down to the children in your life. We talked earlier about embodied healing, involving your body in the healing process. In this moment, imagine holding a basket in your lap of the things your child will need to combat racism. Imagine what these specific things are and what they look like, and then physically begin acting out the gesture of reaching in the basket and first giving these attributes to yourself, by placing your hand from the basket to the top of your head or to your heart, and finally handing these same attributes from your symbolic basket to your children's hands, heart, or head. Consider what you may want to give them: love, clarity, courage, integrity, faith, support, or truth. Take a moment now and physically embody giving the symbolic gifts to yourself and then to your child. As you are doing the exercise, you may want to talk with your child about the values and gifts you want to equip them with so they can be antiracist in the present and in the years to come.

CHAPTER 11

Faith Works: Cultivating Antiracism in Sacred Spaces

Now that you've made steps to adopt an antiracist mindset and apply that mindset in your life, there is an additional area that we invite you to consider: your faith community. One of the criticisms of psychology is that it claims a commitment to holistic health and wellness, but often leaves out spirituality. If you wonder what faith has to do with antiracism, recall the role that people of faith have often played in advocating for racial justice, historically and in the present. In fact, Dr. Christopher Ellison and other researchers in 2008 found that religious attendance, church-based social support, and religious guidance throughout the day help many African Americans offset the distress caused by racism.

Religion is based on an organized set of beliefs and practices shared by a group to foster connection to God and/or the sacred, while spirituality is based on individual purpose, meaning, and connection to that which transcends you. You may believe in one or the other, or you may resonate with being both; either way, your ideas and experiences in this area of your life are part of your psychology. They may help you find meaning, connection, hope, and strength.

Other readers may have had negative experiences with spirituality and religion. It's important to be aware of the ways that faith traditions have been a source of support and resilience and tools of harm.

To begin this chapter, we suggest that you name for yourself your relationship to spirituality and religion.

Please reflect below about the ways in which you're spiritual and/or religious:

_____

_____

_____

_____

_____

For those of you who may have thought that spirituality is separate from race, justice, and politics, we invite you to consider your reflection above as you move throughout this chapter.

SPIRITUALITY, RELIGION, AND RACE

Womanist psychology and multicultural psychology recognize that women and people of color are more likely to indicate that spirituality and religion play an integral role in their meaning-making, worldview, and sense of purpose. Recognizing that people of color are more likely to be spiritual and/or religious, it is important for even readers who do not endorse spirituality or religion to consider the way they think about and perhaps even speak about people of faith. If you automatically assume that people of faith are, for example, ignorant, naive, uncivilized, or brainwashed, it's important to consider the implications of this in terms of your views about people of color. Being dismissive of experiences and beliefs that others hold central to their lives can promote oppressive attitudes and behaviors toward those communities.

Let us consider together the ways that we can mindfully promote antiracism in our personal and collective faith journeys.

Do You See What I See?

In the first part of this book, we spoke about the connections between power, privilege, and racism. For many of you, the greatest power may be your Higher Power or God. For those of you who are spiritual but agnostic or atheist, influence or power may be associated with people you consider great spiritual teachers, writers, or leaders.

Most of us grew up with images of God being a White man. This is so pervasive that it is disturbing for some to see God depicted in artwork as a person of color, and it can be even more startling if the image is of a woman of color.

Please reflect in the space below how you saw God or the divine as a child, and how you see them now. If you've never believed in a Higher Power, reflect perhaps on the image of a spiritual role model, when you were a child and in the present. Additionally, consider the race of that person.

We invite you to reflect below on the race, ethnicity, and gender of this figure, and the impact that image had on your thinking:

_____

_____

_____

_____

_____

As you reflect on what you have written above, we invite you to consider how bringing antiracism to your views of spirituality and/or religion may broaden or even disrupt your notions of the sacred. Also, keep in mind the ripple effect of only seeing God or a spiritual role model as a White man. This can be an unacknowledged manifestation of White supremacy, where Whiteness is the supreme power and source of goodness and sin and evil are connected with images of people of color.

Liberating your view of God and goodness may allow you to see the sacred reflected in every person and race—not only for White people but also many BIPOC who were raised only with images of a White God and White Savior. If you've never seen the divine depicted in diverse races, we encourage you to look online for artwork of God(s) and angels in the image of people who have been racially marginalized. Notice within yourself the feelings and thoughts that come to mind when you see these images.

This stretching in the sacred space is a powerful antiracism act. Cultural racism restricts our thinking and can make it more likely to believe in a White Santa or messiah figure than to believe that the greatest source of power and love could be embodied in the image of a Black person, an Indigenous person, or another person of color.

As we noted in the previous chapter, antiracism doesn't just occur in interpersonal interactions but can also take place in our communities when we shift our policies and practices. Our religious and spiritual practices, as they relate to racism and antiracism, may be grounded in three types of faith and spiritual communities: silent sanctuaries, racism-promoting spaces, and liberating sacred spaces. As we move through describing these faith and spiritual communities, we ask that you reflect on which category your community falls in, and ways you can participate in creating or deepening the antiracism work within that space.

Silent Sanctuaries

Many religious and spiritual communities believe that sacred space should be devoid of politics. They see injustice and other sources of stress and trauma as a distraction from connection with the divine. This can be seen from churches that never mention current events because of a belief that only the Bible should be discussed, to yoga studios that promote the idea that detachment from the outside world is the ultimate path to well-being.

These spaces and those of you who spend time in them may not readily see any harm being done by the silence. You may even feel drawn to these spaces because you want to escape the toxicity of the world around you.

But as we see it, there are two primary harms of this silence. The first is that it leaves those targeted by racism and other forms of injustice lacking support.

Imagine your community is being terrorized and you run into a place full of people smiling and singing. The leaders of these people get up and teach about how it's important to stay positive and not focus on negativity. You leave that place week after week and continue to be terrorized. Would you truly feel that this place is giving you sanctuary? Silent sanctuaries can leave victims of racism and other forms of trauma feeling abandoned, unsupported, unseen, and fundamentally unsafe.

The second major harm of these places is the hypocrisy being taught and modeled within them. When racism is pervasive in the world and is perpetually harming people, silence is cold, fear-based, self-focused, unjust, and oblivious. Living the principles of one's faith requires living the values of compassion, courage, generosity, fairness, and awareness.

As you consider breaking out of or working to transform silent sanctuaries, let's try this cognitive (thought) exercise below. You can change the way you think by challenging and replacing distorted or limiting thoughts.

In the chart below, counter each limiting thought and then propose a new perspective.

Limiting Thought	Argument Against It	Replacement Thought
Religious and spiritual spaces should stay out of politics.		
If people focused on God or spirituality, they wouldn't be so bothered by racism.		
Discussing racism is divisive and the point of faith is to bring people together.		
People come to spiritual spaces for peace. If we start talking about controversial topics, everyone will leave.		

As you reflect on the exercise above, you may find yourself wondering if there is some middle ground. Perhaps you can see the harm of silence, but you also don't want your religious or spiritual place to become another source of stress. The reality is, there are ways to hold both the sacredness of the place and the life challenges, including racism, that people within these spaces are being affected by.

The following are some ways to integrate antiracism within sacred services and programs:

1. During public prayers, you can name racism and pray for justice, safety, and healing for all affected by it.

2. During the sermon or teaching, you can apply the principle of the day to relevant national events. For example, if the topic is compassion, what does it mean to show compassion to those facing anti-Asian harassment?

3. If you take up an offering or collect funds to support the maintenance of the space or organization, you can donate part of the funds to organizations that are working for racial justice or working to serve those whose lives have been devastated as a result of racism.

4. In your sacred space, you can make it a priority to integrate racial diversity in the leadership team, the members who are celebrated, the artwork that is present, and the music that is played.

5. If there is a part of your service or program that includes written or spoken announcements, you can share with the community some events that are happening in your area related to racial justice.

6. Your faith community can build partnerships with other faith communities that are predominantly of another race, perhaps a combined service or a fun social activity.

7. You can encourage members to vote and to vote for policies and politicians that promote equity and not racism.

8. If the teacher or minister recommends books, consider asking them to include a book written by someone of your faith tradition who is discussing racism and/or social justice.

As you read the list above, please note if any seem like a good idea and if any others make you uncomfortable. Reflect in the box below on how the feelings that you experienced represent a connection or disconnection from the antiracism mindset you cultivated in the prior parts of the handbook.

_____

_____

_____

_____

_____

Then, please select one action from the list above to consider trying, and reflect in the space below on any barriers you might confront to completing the action, and ways you may address those barriers.

_____

_____

_____

_____

This reflection was important because, ideally, we all would like to live in alignment with our values. We want an antiracism mindset to manifest in antiracism actions, even in the spiritual spheres of our lives.

If you attend but are not the leader of a silent sanctuary, I invite you to brainstorm and perhaps even role-play ways you could approach the leadership of your community about any of the previously listed suggestions. Would you feel comfortable speaking to those who are in charge, or writing an email or letter?

In addition to describing the suggestion to leadership, you may want to consider: (1) if there is anything that they are doing that you appreciate; (2) a reason you believe the requested action is important, possibly including how it connects with the stated values of the community; and (3) if you would feel more supported if you made the request with the support of some other members or attendees. Additionally, if you're a part of the community, your request is usually more likely to be heard than if it's seen as an outside critique of the community. When seeking to transform spaces, it can be helpful to make more than one request, as you'll likely not get everything you ask for.

Racism-Promoting Spaces

Anusha Wijeyakumar, an antiracism yoga teacher in California, wrote an article in the October 6, 2020 edition of _In Style_ magazine entitled, "We Need to Talk About the Rise of White Supremacy in Yoga." In the article, she describes how the sacred Indian practice has been used to spread racism, which is fundamentally against the teachings of yoga. She gives an example of a lead instructor who has been vocal in the All Lives Matter movement, a movement to counter the Black Lives Matter movement. While not all wellness teachers in the area agreed with this instructor, the majority remained painfully silent.

Anusha describes the experience of many Black and Brown practitioners and teachers who report experiencing overt and covert racism within the wellness community. As opposed to the argument by some that Anusha and others are politicizing the wellness space, Anusha argues that appropriating yoga (divorcing it from its cultural roots), ignoring or denying the deaths of Black people, and tokenizing and humiliating racially marginalized people in yoga spaces is at odds with the foundational teachings of yoga, which teach that we must recognize and honor the divine nature of others through social justice.

A racism-promoting faith community is one that actively promotes and endorses racist people, practices, and policies. These spaces often veil White supremacy in scripture or spiritual teachings that blame those who have been oppressed. These spaces teach hate, fear, and religious arrogance. If you attend these spaces, you're supporting racism with your time, attention, and funds. These are the same groups that stormed The Capitol in 2021 with signs proclaiming they represented Jesus.

Often the messages may be subtle, but they clearly promote hate, fear, and erasure of racially marginalized people and/or immigrants. For example, when racially motivated hate crimes occur in the community and the faith space does not even mention it, the message is sent that the victims' lives do not matter and are not deserving of space in the sacred service.

It's important to recognize these messages when you hear them. We'll list a few below and then invite you to add to the list.

1. Yoga studios that never discuss the cultural roots of yoga.

2. Yoga and meditation studios that only celebrate White bodies.

3. Religious communities that praise political leaders who have endorsed and promoted racism.

4. Religious communities that only discuss people of color as people needing to be saved or rescued, never seeing them as people to learn from and honor.

Use the space below to add examples of faith communities that reinforce the racial hierarchy and racist practice and policies:

_____

_____

_____

_____

_____

_____

These spaces are very resistant to change, but there are those who seek to change them from the inside out. If you're a teacher, you can be intentional about naming, acknowledging, sharing space with, and promoting the leadership of racially underrepresented people and communities. If you're not the leader but an attendee, you can speak with those in leadership or write to them about your concerns. You can build an informal network of antiracist people who are in the community and together you can come up with ways to promote antiracism to others. If you decide to work toward change within a community that is not committed to antiracism, please be careful to (1) monitor what, if anything, your silence is condoning; (2) be aware of the difference between patience with slow progress and enabling racism; and (3) find outside spaces to refresh your spirit so you have the support to continue with your efforts.

Liberating Sacred Spaces

One of the coauthors was invited by Mother Emmanuel AME Church in Charleston, South Carolina, to conduct a workshop on healing the wounds of racism, in the aftermath of the massacre of nine members by a self-proclaimed White supremacist. The pastor described the trauma of the congregation and the Charleston community as well as the outpouring of support the church members received from people of diverse faiths. The daylong workshop and the series of programs the church has had before the massacre and in its aftermath have centered the connection between faith, justice, and liberation. This is aligned with the denomination's founding in 1816, started by Richard Allen and other Black congregants who experienced racial discrimination within the predominantly White church. They created the African Methodist Episcopal (AME) Church to be a place of sacred communion with God and active resistance to racial oppression.

The third type of spiritual space is those that are liberation-oriented and have taken up the baton from the faith communities of the past who courageously fought to dismantle racism—from abolitionist movements to the civil rights movement to contemporary voter engagement movements. These spaces speak and preach about antiracism and follow up with organizing efforts to disrupt racism. The community not only works to raise consciousness among members, but also in the larger community. They may collaborate with racial justice initiatives by sharing resources such as finances and space as well as participates in protests, petitions, and advocacy for justice and equity. They may hold workshops on resistance actions and political mobilization while not only encouraging voting and policy reform but also monitoring the political process and holding accountable politicians who break the trust of the community that put them into office.

These spaces can be refreshing, especially for activists who have felt they had to leave parts of themselves out of other spaces. Some political spaces do not want to hear about spirituality and some silent sanctuaries don't want to hear about racial justice. It can be liberating to be in spaces that welcome the various aspects of your identity.

It's important to note that antiracism among faith communities can also be collaborative and cross the borders of religious or spiritual orientation. This was seen in beautiful ways during the civil rights movement of the 1960s. Great examples from contemporary times include the interfaith religious and spiritual leaders who have come together to protest in support of Black Lives Matter and Stop Asian Hate rallies. Another example is the exchange program with First AME Church, a historically Black congregation in Los Angeles that has been a sociopolitical response center to addressing anti-Black racism, and Temple Isaiah, a progressive Jewish community. At one service each year, the rabbi speaks at the church and the pastor speaks at the synagogue. Additionally, the communities came together virtually during COVID-19, for dialogue and healing from the wounds of racism and antisemitism.

In the space below, write a reflection on your experience with each of the three spiritual spaces we've discussed. What drew you to those spaces, what made you stay, and if you left, what caused you to walk away?

Types of Spiritual Spaces You Have Attended	What Drew You to the Space	What Made You Stay	What, If Anything, Caused You to Leave
Silent Sanctuaries			
Racism-Promoting Spaces			
Liberating Sacred Spaces			

We appreciate you taking time to reflect on your journey toward integrating your spirituality and/or religion and your antiracism commitments. Since this section of the book is about moving from mindset to action, please use the space below to make a commitment to one way you're willing to actively work to bring antiracism to your spiritual or religious life:

_____

_____

_____

Religious/Spiritual Case Study #1

A dissertation study completed by Dr. Marian Fredal in 2008 analyzed an antiracism initiative in the Catholic Church. The study found that the diocese being studied had the commitment and insight to confront racism, whereas most other dioceses have not attempted to actively adopt antiracism. The antiracism initiative first included orientation and training for clergy leaders and the issuing of a statement on diversity and racism to the diocese from church leaders.

The successes of the program included the diocesan commitment to antiracism, the decision to engage in concrete antiracist action, the conduction of listening projects, and the creation and implementation of an atonement ritual, to spiritually address the harms that have been done by racism.

The obstacles to the initiative included individual and institutional racism, challenges with the development of the initiative design, and power struggles over who had control of which aspects of the initiative. Additional challenges included fear, inertia, leadership issues, lack of evaluation development, limited sustainability efforts, and the history between people of color and White people in the diocese.

The researcher concluded that faith-based antiracism is possible, though difficult, and must include people of color in decision-making as well as engage in repair work where ruptures have and will occur. This initiative included hundreds of individuals, and many of them reported being changed by the experience.

Examples of other faith-based antiracism initiatives can be found at faithandlearning.com.

Religious/Spiritual Case Study #2

Another dissertation conducted by Dr. Janet Batacharya in 2011 examined the use of embodied healing and particularly yoga with fifteen young South Asian women, in the form of twelve workshops to address healing from the mental, physical, emotional, and spiritual wounds of violence and oppression. The developers and teachers of the program actively and intentionally resisted New Age interpretations of yoga in terms of individualism, cultural appropriation, and in denial of social inequities. Instead, yoga was framed as an antiracism, feminist, decolonizing, and indigenizing embodiment mechanism for healing. Outcomes from the research interviews with participants in the workshops indicated that embodied practices, specifically yoga, were experienced as helpful as an anti-oppression resource and preferred to other practices that ignored oppression. Respondents reported appreciation for health and healing pathways that attended to the inequities that they faced.

Loving-Kindness Meditation

As we close this chapter and this part, we invite you to take time to refuel by sharing some affirmations, hopes, or prayers for yourself and others who are working to promote antiracism and ultimately liberation. Please open your heart, mind, and spirit, and consider your racial identity and antiracism commitment, as you complete the following sentences (for example, May we have justice and peace, May we have courage to speak truth, May we offer each other authentic sanctuary, May we know deeply that our lives matter and that we are loved).

May we _____

May we _____

May we _____

PART 4

Refilling Your Well: Being Antiracist Is a Long-Term Commitment

At this point in the journey, we hope your toolbox is filled with ideas and strategies for applying antiracism in the diverse areas of your life. While attending a rally, seeing a particularly egregious act of racism, reading a book like this one, or hearing an inspirational speaker can sometimes energize us to activate, the reality is that from time to time, you'll get tired. Fatigue, discouragement, and frustration are all part of the experience of living a life of antiracism. There will be setbacks, delays, and times when it is challenging to see the impact of your efforts.

In these times, it is important to have space to recover and strategies to stay engaged or to re-engage. In this next and final chapter, we will give some perspective and activities that can nourish you and help you to sustain the momentum of your engagement. As you read in the prior section, there is much work to do, and in this chapter, you'll learn how to engage in self-care and community-care so you can have some staying power. We hope this will not be a passing interest for you, but instead that you'll commit to the long road of living a life of antiracism in which justice and liberation are always the aims.

CHAPTER 12

Sustainability:
The Marathon Continues

We are so glad you stayed with us through this process of developing an antiracism mindset and practice. We hope each chapter of this handbook has brought you insights and practical strategies. And while we are excited about the work you've done and the ways you'll contribute to antiracism and liberation, it's important that we prepare you for the road ahead.

Uprooting racism and challenging White supremacy do not happen overnight; the work requires resilience and endurance. We are making a point to celebrate your commitment to antiracism because the unfortunate reality is that not everyone will be pleased with your efforts toward racial justice and equity. You'll likely encounter resistance and roadblocks along the way. But you can sustain your commitment by being aware of those obstacles to progress as you keep moving forward.

As hip-hop artist, activist, and entrepreneur Ermias Asghedom, known as Nipsey Hussle, noted: "The marathon continues." This is not a sprint, so we hope you'll have staying power and remain engaged in the struggle to achieve justice and equity. Your antiracism practice can be part of a legacy of racial and social justice activism that has spanned generations. To empower you to stay committed and engaged, we would like to spend this concluding chapter focusing on *sustainability*, and letting you know what to expect in terms of challenges and how to prevent and address burnout when it occurs.

To prepare for the challenges of sustaining antiracism engagement, it helps to "remember your why," or the reasons you took those first steps in this work, and the potential benefits of your engagement. In Dr. Bryant's work with Dr. Comas-Díaz, activism is described as a potential resource of empowerment, agency, self-definition, and transformation. In the space below, please reflect on what you've gained so far in your antiracism journey. Benefits may include a renewed sense of hope, empowerment, connection to others, values-based living, and seeing improvements in yourself, your community, and the systems in which you engage.

_____

_____

_____

_____

_____

_____

_____

Look back on what you're written about the benefits you've gained through your antiracist engagement. Allow yourself to recognize and acknowledge the good work you've done and the ways you've grown because of your efforts. Affirming yourself can be nourishment for your spirit as you sustain your antiracist practice. Come back to this section to remind yourself of all that you've gained when you feel tired or when your commitment is wavering.

In our next part, we're going to talk more about the fatigue you may experience as part of your antiracist practice and the real danger of burnout that may arise as well.

RACIAL BATTLE FATIGUE AND ACTIVISM BURNOUT

As we mentioned in the first part of this handbook, racism is both historical and ongoing. This reality means that we are not only just working to address injustices of the past but also working to combat racism as it continues to manifest in our lives. Instead of living in a "post-racial" world where racial trauma no longer exists, we are living with continuous racial stress and trauma. As a result, you'll need to take special care of yourself—mind, body, and spirit—as you confront racial stress and trauma. You'll be affected by racism in general, whether racism that you are the target of or vicarious racial trauma that you witness or learn about from loved ones or through the media. You are also likely to experience racial battle fatigue.

Racial battle fatigue is a term coined by education professor and critical race theorist William Smith. He initially developed racial battle fatigue as a concept with the experience of Black people in mind, but it has been expanded to encompass the potential experience of all people of color. According to Smith (2008), racial battle fatigue is the cumulative result of race-related stress responses emerging "from constantly facing racially dismissive, demeaning, insensitive, and/or hostile racial environments and individuals." Psychologist Robert Carter and his colleagues (2020) added that if you're a BIPOC and have been in predominantly White spaces in which you've felt threatened or unsafe, you may have experienced a number of symptoms of distress including but not limited to:

- Anxiety

- Racing heart

- Sweating

- Insomnia

- Tension headaches

- Jumpiness

- Social withdrawal

- Compromised immune system or getting sick more frequently

- High blood pressure

- Difficulty thinking and/or speaking clearly

In the space below, please reflect on experiences you've had either while confronting racism, in the aftermath of leaving a space where racism was very evident, or in preparation for having to enter such spaces. While racial battle fatigue was developed with BIPOC in mind, if you're White and have experienced a physical or emotional response in spaces where you observed racism, you may also reflect on your experiences below.

_____

_____

_____

_____

_____

_____

Activism Burnout

Along with racism-related stress, you may also experience *activism burnout*, which is distress and fatigue resulting from engaging in antiracism practice or activism. Engaging in antiracism activism may increase your visibility and therefore your vulnerability to racist attacks. Activists may be targeted, ridiculed, rejected, and vilified by the media, police officers, family members, "friends," those benefiting from racist policies, and members of White supremacist organizations. According to multicultural education professor Dr. Paul Gorski (2019), activism can have psychological, social, and financial costs, while research from education and psychology professor Elan Hope and colleagues (2018) found that Black people engaging in political activism faced more racially motivated microaggressions than Black people who didn't engage in such activities. We described the psychological costs of facing racial microaggressions and stress earlier; they include depression, anxiety, rage, and feeling overwhelmed. Social costs to antiracist activism may include isolation and rejection, while financial costs may include needing to use your funds to support antiracism efforts, having to pay bail or legal fees for yourself or others, having to pay for security, losing a job, or being passed over for a promotion as a result of speaking up about racism. If you've already begun to go beyond developing an antiracist mindset and have put the strategies in this handbook in practice, please reflect below on any costs you've experienced.

Psychological/Emotional Costs	1.
	2.
	3.
Social Costs	1.
	2.
	3.

Financial Costs	1.
	2.
	3.

As you look at the costs and consequences you've faced, you may have mixed feelings. You may feel angry, disappointed, sad, surprised, or even embarrassed if you feel you haven't done enough. Wherever you are on the journey, it's important to have the self-awareness and compassion to begin, or continue, moving forward. Please refer to the chart above as you use the space below to reflect on how you feel about your antiracism efforts in relation to the consequences you've experienced.

_____

_____

_____

_____

_____

_____

_____

Our purpose in having you reflect on some of the costs of antiracist activism and the related feelings you've experienced is for you to become aware of the ways that sustained antiracist practice can be a challenge. You may experience burnout or weariness physically, emotionally, and spiritually. We want you to try and recognize when this is happening so that you know your limits and when you'll need to put strategies in place to sustain your commitment and restore your well-being.

STRATEGIES TO SUSTAIN YOUR ANTIRACISM PRACTICE

Cultivate Positive Racial Identity and Sense of Community

Earlier in this handbook, we emphasized the need to understand racial identity—or how important race is to your sense of self. We hope those earlier reflection questions and exercises helped you get a clearer idea of what your racial identity meant for you as you began to think more deeply about antiracist practice.

Please take a moment now to review what you wrote about your racial identity when you first began this handbook. Then think about how your sense of self, as it relates to race and your racial group membership(s), has been influenced as you continued reading and engaging with this handbook.

Your racial identity can serve as a wonderful resource for you as you continue your antiracist engagement. For BIPOC readers especially, think about how being a part of your racial groups has been a source of pride and connection to a rich legacy. Whether through music, books, or other expressions of creativity and knowledge that your community has crafted, or the food that has nourished you and your family across generations, your racial identity can serve as a resource as you continue your antiracist practice.

For those of our White readers who may be struggling with thinking of racial identity as a resource, we suggest you reflect on the history of White allies who have contributed to the fight for racial justice and draw upon the lessons from their lived experience for inspiration.

While we experience racial identity as individuals, it is shaped by the interactions and relationships we have as part of our community. We believe that cultivating a sense of community will also help to sustain your antiracist engagement. In their seminal piece, "Sense of Community: A Definition and Theory," community psychologists David McMillan and David Chavis (1986) define a sense of community as the "feeling that members have of belonging, a feeling that members matter to one another and to the group, and a shared faith that members' needs will be met through their commitment to be together" (9). We can foster and experience a sense of community that nurtures us within and across the groups that make up the key parts of our identity—our racial group(s), gender, and/or sexual orientation, to highlight just a few of our social identities.

What's key about sense of community is that you should be able to bring your whole self to your antiracist practice. Find those communities where you can authentically connect with others who respect and honor all aspects of your identity, and then draw on this resource in sustaining your antiracist engagement.

Body Temple Care

When we are committed to a cause such as antiracism, we often make sacrifices—consciously and unconsciously. One of the first things we sometimes sacrifice is our wellness and care. We're sure you can remember a time when, because you valued a job, a degree, or a loved one, you sacrificed sleep and time to invest in those things or people you care about. Likewise, your commitment to racial justice, combined with witnessing ongoing acts of racism, violent hate crimes, and corrupt systems, can leave you feeling like it is selfish to rest.

There is only so much time you can spend ignoring your body temple before the murmurs of discomfort become full screams of sickness or depletion. To maintain your commitment to antiracist engagement requires that you maintain a commitment to your physical wellness.

You may be the kind of person that doesn't take a break until you break down. That lifestyle is not sustainable. Not only does self-neglect sabotage your commitment to antiracism practice, but according to Tricia Hersey, known as The Nap Bishop and founder of The Nap Ministry, neglecting the body is actually a function of racism and capitalism, which teaches us that we are not deserving of rest. To be antiracist is to honor your humanity and rest when you need to. We invite you to take a moment to reflect on that point.

What will it mean to make rest and self-care a part of your commitment to antiracism and anti-oppression overall? You may want to specifically reflect on (1) the messages you received directly and indirectly about your being deserving of rest, and (2) your image/fantasy of an antiracist person, as it relates to balance and rest.

_____

_____

_____

_____

_____

_____

Accountability is helpful when we want to make lifestyle changes, so we invite you to complete the chart below, where you'll assess your current level of and optimum goals for self-care. Writing it down and occasionally coming back to review this chapter can be helpful. Additionally, sharing your intentions with a friend or therapist may also help you to be more accountable for these commitments. Complete the chart as honestly and realistically as you can. (For example, if you currently get five hours of sleep a night, to say that starting tonight you'll sleep nine hours a night may set you up for failure.) Try to set goals that will challenge you but that are attainable and maintainable.

	Current Reality	Goal/Commitment	One Thing That Will Help Me Make the Change
Nutrition (on a typical day) For example: types of food you want to choose or refrain from; not eating after a certain time of day; replacing emotional eating (from anxiety, depression, boredom, etc.) with a wellness activity like journaling or walking			
Drinking water			

Sleep			
Exercise			

Liberate Your Mental Health

Being engaged in antiracism may deplete you not only physically but also emotionally. It's important to take care of your mental health. To decolonize psychology is in part to recognize the impact that injustice has on your wellness and to actively work to resist the distressing, toxic messages of oppressive systems such as racism. While we shared an entire unit on psychological barriers to engaging in antiracism, it is also important to note the psychological costs of this work. In the space below, reflect on the following:

1. How has engaging in antiracism affected you emotionally?

    _____

    _____

2. How has it affected your concentration or focus?

    _____

    _____

3. How has it affected any preexisting mental health challenges you live with (for example, depression, childhood trauma, substance dependence, disordered eating, etc.)?

    _____

    _____

    _____

Recognizing these effects is one aspect of liberating or decolonizing your mental health. Another strategy is reclaiming, or claiming for the first time, Indigenous healing practices. BIPOC readers and White readers can research their ethnic heritage and learn about wellness practices and traditions from their ancestors. These practices may include cultural songs, dances, meals, crafts, or spiritual rituals. It is important to explore your ethnic heritage instead of falsely assuming that your heritage either holds no value (internalized oppression) or is nonexistent (e.g., White people such as Italian Americans, Jewish Americans, etc. who have not been taught anything about their ethnic heritage).

Consider your ethnic background. This applies to White readers as well. In the space below, consider cultural resources that people from your racial and/or ethnic group have used to refresh themselves or cope with stress and trauma in healthy ways. Note cultural traditions you're aware of and then whether you've adopted them or are open to exploring them. They may not all resonate with you, but the ones that do can be great sources of utilizing culture as medicine.

	Cultural Tradition from My Race/Ethnic Group	My Relationship to This Tradition—Have Used in Past or Am Open to Exploring in Future
Arts and Crafts		
Spirituality		
Community Gathering (formally or informally)		
Comfort Foods		
Community Role Models and Elders		
Oral Tradition (storytelling, etc.)		
If you have an idea (or find one) that was not listed above, describe it in this row:		

Take a moment to reflect on what reflecting on your cultural traditions was like for you. Could you readily complete the chart? Did you need to search the Internet or consult with another member of your community? We encourage you to push through any frustration, to find customs that align with you as you seek to connect to heritage.

Another strategy to liberate your mental health is journaling. There is a lot of psychological research to support the benefits of journaling, especially in the face of stress and trauma. James Pennebaker, a social psychologist, has written a lot about the ways expressive writing can improve your health and relieve emotional pain. You can begin to keep a journal on your reactions to your process with this handbook as well as your experiences with your antiracism commitments going forward.

EXERCISE: Visualizing Your Own Path to Wellness

Sometimes we have mental blocks to the idea of journaling. Some of the objections we have heard in the past include "When I was a child, someone found my journal and I vowed I would never write again," or "I'm not a good writer." A part of your liberation may be reclaiming your pen, your voice, and your right to write. We would like to offer this visualization exercise.

1. Cross your arms over your chest so that each hand is touching the opposite shoulder, if that feels okay with you. This is called a butterfly hold and is used in some eye movement desensitization therapy (EMDR) as well as in some yoga practices.

2. From this position of comfort, say to yourself "My story is important." Or "My thoughts are important." Or "My journey is important."

3. Now we invite you to close your eyes and see yourself writing. The negative thoughts and feelings may come up, but explore what it feels like in your body to imagine that you have the freedom and comfort to write your thoughts.

Take a moment to breathe as you lower your arms and reflect on what that visualization was like for you. You are the author of your story, so if journaling seems like something you're open to trying, we encourage you to explore it. If you feel like it is not the pathway for you, we encourage you to honor that and continue to explore other paths to wellness.

Social Justice–Oriented Therapy

The last mental health strategy we will mention for sustaining your antiracist engagement is therapy, and in particular, therapy with a social justice–oriented therapist. If you try therapy and the therapist is clearly uncomfortable attending to racism, antiracism, or activism, you'll likely want to find another therapist to help you with racism-related stress and trauma. There are a number of directories that are specific to BIPOC mental health professionals including but not limited to:

Latinxtherapy.com

Inclusivetherapists.com

Melaninandmentalhealth.com

Therapyforblackgirls.com

Southasiantherapists.org

Therapyforqpoc.com

Therapythatliberates.com

We encourage our BIPOC readers to resist the idea that therapy is only for White people, rich people, or people with "more serious" problems than you. You are worthy of care. Each of us is worthy of care.

If you're already in or have been in therapy and racism was never discussed, we encourage you to share with your current or future therapist your desire to receive support for the work you're doing around antiracism. If they are open to it, try to be as honest as possible in sharing the ways you've been affected by antiracism work. If they are not receptive or helpful, we want you to know that there are therapists who are more oriented to antiracism, so don't hesitate to shop around until you find a good fit. As you think about the possibility of starting, continuing, or returning to therapy, please complete the chart below, which can help you to move forward.

	Barrier to Seeking Therapy in This Area	Potential Therapy Benefit in This Area
Emotional		
Financial		
Time		
Cultural		
Spiritual		

As you review the chart above, take a moment to reflect on your decision to pursue therapy at this time, postpone it, or decide not to go. Reflect in the space below about your decision, considering how, if at all, it relates to antiracism.

_____

_____

_____

_____

_____

FEEDING YOUR SPIRIT

A part of our commitment as culturally attuned psychologists is a commitment to holistic care, inclusive of body, heart, mind, culture, and spirit. In alignment with this value, we could not end this book without inviting you to consider affirmative sacred practices that can nourish you on your antiracism journey. Many people who have engaged in liberation movements have been inspired by their faith, spirituality, and/or religion. As we consider the vastness of the challenge, we know that doing this work requires hope that we can achieve more than we have ever seen in the arena of racial justice. We would like to offer three spiritual practices that may ground you in this work and give you momentum to engage.

The first activity we call *sacred pause*. This is a moment for stillness and silence, to focus in on your inner resource. Whether that resource is the creator, your ancestors, role models, values, or yourself, we encourage you to take a few minutes each day to shift from the busy pace of your daily life and center in. For some of you, that may take the form of meditation, for others it may be prayer, and for others, it may be reflecting on gratitude or envisioning what justice looks and feels like. The important part about sacred pause is making it a regular practice that can be done daily or multiple times throughout the day. In the space below, simply jot down what time(s) you would like to take sacred pause and perhaps the amount of time you want to give to it—whatever feels right for you.

_____

_____

_____

The second activity for feeding your spirit is *reading a sacred or inspirational text*—a holy book, poetry collection, memoir, or any text that inspires you. Reading sacred or inspirational texts can achieve a number of goals, including:

1. Reminding you that you're not alone on this journey

2. Providing motivation and inspiration to continue

3. Providing strategies for your care or your engagement

4. Giving you hope for the future

In the space below, write the names of three books or three authors that you find inspiring or spiritually nourishing:

1. _____

2. _____

3. _____

If you do not know any, give yourself the gift of being open to finding some. If you've completed this workbook, but usually don't consider yourself a reader, you may want to try audiobooks or podcasts for inspiration.

The third spiritual practice is *embodied healing*, which we have invited you to engage in a few times on this journey. From time to time, you may want to play an inspiring or spiritually nourishing song and give your body temple the gift of self-massage in places where you usually hold tension: your neck, shoulders, lower back, forehead, or any area where you feel the stress of the day. If you've never engaged in self-massage, consider trying circular motions, pressing and releasing with your thumbs, or sliding your hands downward. Taking a moment to recall the sacred gift of your life and body is a great way to release stress and shift your focus.

RENEWED MIND, RENEWED MISSION

Welcome to the next chapter of your antiracism practice. The pen is in your hands. We hope you write something on the pages of your life that reflects antiracism and promotes liberation within yourself, your community, and the larger world. There will be challenges along the way, but you can learn from those and apply them as you continue doing the work. Engaging in antiracism does not require perfection, but it will require persistence. Count and celebrate your wins along the way. Don't quit. Rest, restore, and reengage.

Thank you for taking this journey with us!

References

Alvarez, A. N., C. T. H. Liang, and H. A. Neville, eds. 2016. *The Cost of Racism for People of Color: Contextualizing Experiences of Discrimination.* American Psychological Association, Cultural, Racial, and Ethnic Psychology Book Series. https://doi.org/10.1037/14852-000.

Anderson, R. E., and H. C. Stevenson. 2019. "RECASTing Racial Stress and Trauma: Theorizing the Healing Potential of Racial Socialization in Families." *American Psychologist* 74(1): 63–75.

Arminio, J. 2001. "Exploring the Nature of Race-Related Guilt." *Journal of Multicultural Counseling and Development* 29(4): 239–252. https://doi-org.lib.pepperdine.edu/10.1002/j.2161-1912.2001.tb00467.x.

Bartoli, E., A. Michael, K. L. Bentley-Edwards, H. C. Stevenson, R. E. Shor, and S. E. McClain. 2016. "Training for Colour-Blindness: White Racial Socialisation." *Whiteness and Education* 1(2): 125–136.

Batacharya, J. S. 2011. "Life in a Body: Counter Hegemonic Understandings of Violence, Oppression, Healing and Embodiment among Young South Asian Women." In *Dissertation Abstracts International* Section A: Humanities and Social Sciences, vol. 72, issue 6–A: 1954. ProQuest Information and Learning.

Blodorn, A., and L. T. O'Brien. 2011. "Perceptions of Racism in Hurricane Katrina–Related Events: Implications for Collective Guilt and Mental Health among White Americans." *Analyses of Social Issues and Public Policy (ASAP)* 11(1): 127–140.

Bryant-Davis, T., and L. Comas-Díaz. 2016. "Introduction: Womanist and Mujerista Psychologies." In *Womanist and Mujerista Psychologies: Voices of Fire, Acts of Courage:* 3–25. Washington, D.C.: American Psychological Association.

Cabrera, N. L. 2017. White Immunity: Working through Some of the Pedagogical Pitfalls of "Privilege." *JCSCORE* 3(1): 77–90.

Carter, R. T., K. Kirkinis, and V. E. Johnson. 2020. "Relationships between Trauma Symptoms and Race-Based Traumatic Stress." *Traumatology* 26(1): 11–18.

Case, K. A., J. Iuzzini, and M. Hopkins. 2012. "Systems of Privilege: Intersections, Awareness, and Applications." *Journal of Social Issues* 68(1), 1–10.

Comas-Díaz, L. 2016. "Racial Trauma Recovery: A Race-Informed Therapeutic Approach to Racial Wounds." In *The Cost of Racism for People of Color: Contextualizing Experiences of Discrimination*, edited by A. N. Alvarez, C. T. H. Liang, and H. A. Neville: 249–272. Washington, DC: American Psychological Association. Cultural, Racial, and Ethnic Psychology book series.

Crenshaw, K. 2016. "The Urgency of Intersectionality." Retrieved from https://www.ted.com/talks/kimberle_crenshaw_the_urgency_of_intersectionality.

Cross, W. E., Jr. 1991. *Shades of Black: Diversity in African-American Identity.* Philadelphia: Temple University Press.

Daley, J. 2021. "Killings by Police Declined After Black Lives Matter Protests." *Scientific American.* Retrieved from https://www.scientificamerican.com/article/killings-by-police-declined-after-black-lives-matter-protests1/.

Diemer, M. A., A. Kauffman, N. Koenig, E. Trahan, and C.A. Hsieh. 2006. "Challenging Racism, Sexism, and Social Injustice: Support for Urban Adolescents' Critical Consciousness Development." *Cultural Diversity and Ethnic Minority Psychology* 12(3): 444–460.

Dupree, C. H., B. Torrez, O. Obioha, and S. T. Fiske. 2020. "Race-Status Associations: Distinct Effects of Three Novel Measures among White and Black Perceivers." *Journal of Personality and Social Psychology.*

Eberhardt, J. L. 2019. *Biased: Uncovering the Hidden Prejudice That Shapes What We See, Think, and Do.* New York: Viking.

Ellison, C. G., M. A. Musick, and A. K. Henderson. 2008. "Balm in Gilead: Racism, Religious Involvement, and Psychological Distress among African-American Adults." *Journal for the Scientific Study of Religion* 47(2): 291–309.

Fine, M., and W. E. Cross, Jr. 2016. "Critical Race, Psychology, and Social Policy: Refusing Damage, Cataloging Oppression, and Documenting Desire." In *The Cost of Racism for People of Color: Contextualizing Experiences of Discrimination*, edited by A. N. Alvarez, C. T. H. Liang, and

H. A. Neville: 273–294. Washington, D.C.: American Psychological Association. Cultural, Racial, and Ethnic Psychology book series.

Flintoff, A., F. Dowling, and H. Fitzgerald. 2015. "Working through Whiteness, Race, and (Anti) Racism in Physical Education Teacher Education." *Physical Education and Sport Pedagogy* 20(5): 559–570.

Fredal, M. 2008. "A Catholic Diocese's Initiative to End Racism: A Case Study." *Dissertation Abstracts International Section A: Humanities and Social Sciences* vol. 68, issue 12–A: 5217.

Gilliam, W. S., A. N. Maupin, C. R. Reyes, M. Accavitti, and F. Shic. 2016. "Do Early Educators' Implicit Biases Regarding Sex and Race Relate to Behavior Expectations and Recommendations of Preschool Expulsions and Suspensions?" *Yale University Child Study Center* 9(28).

Gorski, P. C. 2019. "Fighting Racism, Battling Burnout: Causes of Activist Burnout in US Racial Justice Activists." *Ethnic and Racial Studies* 42(5): 667–687.

Gorski, P. C., and C. Chen. 2015. "'Frayed All Over': The Causes and Consequences of Activist Burnout among Social Justice Education Activists." *Educational Studies: Journal of the American Educational Studies Association* 51(5): 385–405.

Gorski, P.C., and N. Erakat. 2019. "Racism, Whiteness, and Burnout in Antiracism Movements: How White Racial Justice Activists Elevate Burnout in Racial Justice Activists of Color in the United States." *Ethnicities* 19(5): 784–808.

Griffith, D. M., M. Mason, M. Yonas, E. Eng, V. Jeffries, S. Plihcik, and B. Parks. 2007. "Dismantling Institutional Racism: Theory and Action." *American Journal of Community Psychology* 39(3-4): 381–392.

Grzanka, P. R., K. A. Gonzalez, and L. B. Spanierman. 2019. "White Supremacy and Counseling Psychology: A Critical-Conceptual Framework." *The Counseling Psychologist* 47(4): 478–529.

Helms, J. E., ed. 1990. "Contributions in Afro-American and African Studies." *Black and White Racial Identity: Theory, Research, and Practice.* Westport, CT: Greenwood Press.

Hope, E. C., G. Velez, C. Offidani-Bertrand, M. Keels, and M. I. Durkee. 2018. "Political Activism and Mental Health among Black and Latinx College Students." *Cultural Diversity and Ethnic Minority Psychology* 24(1), 26–39.

Horsford, S. 2014. "When Race Enters the Room: Improving Leadership and Learning through Racial Literacy." *Theory Into Practice* 53(2), 123–130.

Hughes, D., J. Rodriguez, E. P. Smith, D. J. Johnson, H. C. Stevenson, and P. Spicer. 2006. "Parents' Ethnic-Racial Socialization Practices: A Review of Research and Directions for Future Study." *Developmental Psychology* 42(5): 747–770. https://doi-org.lib.pepperdine.edu/10.1037/0012-1649 .42.5.747.

Isaacs, S. T. 2011. "Portrayal of African Americans in the Media: An Examination of Law and Order." https://www.semanticscholar.org/paper/Portrayal-of-African-Americans-in-the-Media-% 3A-An-of-Isaacs/83cb50c144ae316e19cee4320a7fb852ef3936ea.

Jackson, S. J., and B. F. Welles. 2016. "#Ferguson Is Everywhere: Initiators in Emerging Counterpublic Networks." *Information, Communication and Society* 19(3): 397–418.

Jones, C. P. 2002. "Confronting Institutionalized Racism." *Phylon (1960-)*: 7–22.

Jones, C. P. 2000. "Levels of Racism: A Theoretic Framework and a Gardener's Tale." *American Journal of Public Health* 90(8): 1212–1215.

Jones, C. P. 2020. "Seeing the Water: Seven Values Targets for Anti-Racism Action." *Harvard Primary Care Blog.* http://info.primarycare.hms.harvard.edu/blog/seven-values-targets-antiracism-action.

Maton, K. I., K. Humphreys, L. A. Jason, and M. Shinn, eds. 2017. "Community Psychology in the Policy Arena." In *APA Handbook of Community Psychology: Methods for Community Research and Action for Diverse Groups and Issues*: 275–295. Washington, D.C.: American Psychological Association.

McGuire, T. G., and J. Miranda. 2008. "New Evidence Regarding Racial and Ethnic Disparities in Mental Health: Policy Implications." *Health Affairs (Project Hope)* 27(2): 393–403.

McIntosh, P. 1988. "White Privilege: Unpacking the Invisible Knapsack." *Peace and Freedom Magazine*, July/August 1989: 10–12.

McMillan, D. W., and D. M. Chavis. 1986. "Sense of Community: A Definition and Theory." *Journal of Community Psychology* 14(1): 6–23.

Menakem, R. 2017. *My Grandmother's Hands: Racialized Trauma and Healing the Heart and Body.* Central Recovery Press: Las Vegas.

Metzl, J. M. 2019. *Dying of Whiteness: How the Politics of Racial Resentment Is Killing America's Heartland.* Basic Books: New York.

National Community Reinvestment Coalition. 2020. "Lending Discrimination within the Paycheck Protection Program." https://www.ncrc.org/lending-discrimination-within-the-paycheck-protection -program/.

Neal, J. W., and Z. P. Neal. 2011. "Power as a Structural Phenomenon." *American Journal of Community Psychology* 48: 157–167.

Nelson, J. K. 2015. "'Speaking' Racism and Antiracism: Perspectives of Local Antiracism Actors." *Ethnic and Racial Studies* 38(2): 342–358.

Ng, W. 2012. "Pedagogy of Solidarity: Educating for an Interracial Working Class Movement." *Journal of Workplace Learning* 24(7–8): 528–537.

Office of the Surgeon General, Center for Mental Health Services, National Institute of Mental Health. 2001. "Mental Health: Culture, Race, and Ethnicity: A Supplement to Mental Health: A Report of the Surgeon General." Rockville, MD: Substance Abuse and Mental Health Services Administration. Chapter 1: Introduction. Available at https://www.ncbi.nlm.nih.gov/books/NBK 44246/.

Parker, G. 2020. *Restorative Yoga for Ethnic and Race-Based Stress and Trauma.* London: Singing Dragon.

Patel, S. G., K. Tabb, and S. Sue. 2017. "Diversity, Multiculturalism, and Inclusion." In *APA Handbook of Community Psychology: Theoretical Foundations, Core Concepts, and Emerging Challenges:* 253–273.

Pearman, F. 2020. "Anti-blackness and the Way Forward for K-12 Schooling." *The Brown Center Chalkboard.* https://www.brookings.edu/blog/brown-center-chalkboard/2020/07/01/anti-blackness -and-the-way-forward-for-k-12-schooling/.

Pew Research Center. 2019. "Race in America 2019." https://www.pewresearch.org/social- trends/2019/04/09/race-in-america-2019/.

Pieterse, A., and S. Powell. 2016. "A Theoretical Overview of the Impact of Racism on People of Color." In *The Cost of Racism for People of Color: Contextualizing Experiences of Discrimination:* 11–30. Washington, D.C.: American Psychological Association. Cultural, Racial, and Ethnic Psychology Book Series.

Pinderhughes, E. 2017. "Conceptualization of How Power Operates in Human Functioning." *Understanding Power: An Imperative for Human Services:* 1–23. https://www.naswpress.org/product /53475/understanding-power.

Pinderhughes, E. 1989. *Understanding Race, Ethnicity, and Power: The Key to Efficacy in Clinical Practice.* New York: Simon and Schuster.

Rios, D., K. A. Case, S. M. Brody, and D. P. Rivera. 2021. "When the Professor Experiences Stereotype Threat in the Classroom." In *Navigating Difficult Moments in Teaching Diversity and Social Justice:* 59–73. Washington, D.C.: American Psychological Association.

Rosales, C., and R. D. Langhout. 2020. "Just Because We Don't See It, Doesn't Mean It's Not There: Everyday Resistance in Psychology." *Social and Personality Psychology Compass* 14(1).

Ross, K. M. 2020. *Call It What It Is: Anti-Blackness. New York Times.* https://www.nytimes.com /2020/06/04/opinion/george-floyd-anti-blackness.html.

Sellers, R. M., M. A. Smith, J. N. Shelton, S. J. Rowley, and T. M. Chavous. 1998. "Multidimensional Model of Racial Identity: A Reconceptualization of African American Racial Identity." *Personality and Social Psychology Review* 2 (1): 18–39.

Smedley, A., and B. D. Smedley. 2005. "Race as Biology Is Fiction, Racism as a Social Problem Is Real: Anthropological and Historical Perspectives on the Social Construction of Race." *American Psychologist* 60(1): 16–26. https://doi.org/10.1037/0003-066X.60.1.16.

Smedley, B. D. 2019. "Multilevel Interventions to Undo the Health Consequences of Racism: The Need for Comprehensive Approaches." *Cultural Diversity and Ethnic Minority Psychology* 25(1): 123–125.

Steele, C. M. 1997. "A Threat in the Air: How Stereotypes Shape Intellectual Identity and Performance." *American Psychologist* 52(6): 613–629.

Stevenson, H. C. 2014. *Promoting Racial Literacy in Schools: Differences That Make a Difference.* New York: Teachers College Press.

Sue, D. W. 2013. "Race Talk: The Psychology of Racial Dialogues." *American Psychologist* 68: 663–672.

Sue, D. W., S. Alsaidi, M. N. Awad, E. Glaeser, C. Z. Calle, and N. Mendez. 2019. "Disarming Racial Microaggressions: Microintervention Strategies for Targets, White Allies, and Bystanders." *American Psychologist* 74(1): 128–142.

Sue, D. W., C. M. Capodilupo, G. C. Torino, J. M. Bucceri, A. M. B. Holder, K. L. Nadal, and M. Esquilin. 2007. "Racial Microaggressions in Everyday Life: Implications for Clinical Practice." *American Psychologist* 62: 271–286.

Tatum, B. D. 2007. *Can We Talk About Race?: And Other Conversations in an Era of School Resegregation.* Boston: Beacon Press.

Tittler, M. V., and N. G. Wade. 2019. "Engaging White Participants in Racial Dialogues: Group Composition and Dialogue Structure." *Group Dynamics: Theory, Research, and Practice,* 23(2): 75–90.

Wellman, D. 2000. "From Evil to Illness: Medicalizing Racism." *American Journal of Orthopsychiatry* 70 (1): 28–32.

Wilkerson, I. 2020. *Caste: The Lies That Divide Us.* New York: Random House.

Williams, D. R., J. A. Lawrence, and B. A. Davis. 2019. "Racism and Health: Evidence and Needed Research." *Annual Review of Public Health* 40: 105–125.

Zack, N. 2015. *White Privilege and Black Rights: The Injustice of US Police Racial Profiling and Homicide.* Lanham, MD: Rowman and Littlefield.

Thema Bryant, PhD, is a licensed psychologist who has worked nationally and globally to provide relief and empowerment to marginalized persons. She is past president of the Society for the Psychology of Women, and past American Psychological Association (APA) representative to the United Nations, as well as the current president-elect of the APA. Bryant has been honored by the APA; the Institute of Violence, Abuse, and Trauma; and the California Psychological Association for her contributions to psychology. A professor at Pepperdine University, she earned her undergraduate and doctorate degrees in psychology from Duke University, and completed her postdoctoral training at Harvard Medical School. Bryant has served as a mental health media consultant for numerous print, radio, and television outlets, and is host of *The Homecoming Podcast*.

Edith G. Arrington, PhD, is a licensed psychologist whose research, writing, and consulting focus on race, identity, development, and education; equity, diversity, and inclusion; and promoting health and well-being for individuals and communities. She has provided a range of professional services, including evaluation, assessment, and strategic planning to schools, families, community-based organizations, and philanthropic organizations. Arrington earned her undergraduate degree in psychology and sociology from Duke University; her master's degree in clinical/community psychology from the University of Virginia; and her doctorate in school, community, and clinical child psychology from the University of Pennsylvania Graduate School of Education.

Foreword writer **Kevin L. Nadal, PhD**, is professor of psychology at both John Jay College of Criminal Justice, and the Graduate Center at the City University of New York. He received his doctorate in counseling psychology from Columbia University. Nadal's research focuses on the impacts of microaggressions on the mental and physical health of marginalized groups.

Real change *is* possible

For more than forty five years, New Harbinger has published proven-effective self-help books and pioneering workbooks to help readers of all ages and backgrounds improve mental health and well-being, and achieve lasting personal growth. In addition, our spirituality books offer profound guidance for deepening awareness and cultivating healing, self-discovery, and fulfillment.

Founded by psychologist Matthew McKay and Patrick Fanning, New Harbinger is proud to be an independent, employee-owned company. Our books reflect our core values of integrity, innovation, commitment, sustainability, compassion, and trust. Written by leaders in the field and recommended by therapists worldwide, New Harbinger books are practical, accessible, and provide real tools for real change.

 **newharbinger**publications

MORE BOOKS from
NEW HARBINGER PUBLICATIONS

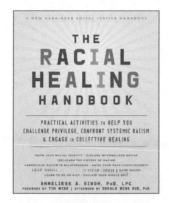

THE RACIAL HEALING HANDBOOK

Practical Activities to Help You Challenge Privilege, Confront Systemic Racism, and Engage in Collective Healing

978-1684032709 / US $24.95

THE FEMINIST HANDBOOK

Practical Tools to Resist Sexism and Dismantle the Patriarchy

978-1684033805 / US $19.95

THE HEALING OTHERNESS HANDBOOK

Overcome the Trauma of Identity-Based Bullying and Find Power in Your Difference

978-1684036479 / US $18.95

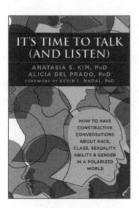

IT'S TIME TO TALK (AND LISTEN)

How to Have Constructive Conversations About Race, Class, Sexuality, Ability, and Gender in a Polarized World

978-1684032679 / US $16.95

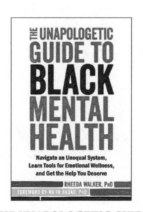

THE UNAPOLOGETIC GUIDE TO BLACK MENTAL HEALTH

Navigate an Unequal System, Learn Tools for Emotional Wellness, and Get the Help you Deserve

978-1684034147 / US $16.95

WHAT MAKES YOU STRONGER

How to Thrive in the Face of Change and Uncertainty Using Acceptance and Commitment Therapy

978-1684038602 / US $18.95

newharbinger**publications

1-800-748-6273 / newharbinger.com

(VISA, MC, AMEX / prices subject to change without notice)

Follow Us 🅾 f 🐦 ▶ 📌 in

Did you know there are **free tools** you can download for this book?

Free tools are things like **worksheets**, **guided meditation exercises**, and **more** that will help you get the most out of your book.

You can download free tools for this book—whether you bought or borrowed it, in any format, from any source—from the New Harbinger website. All you need is a NewHarbinger.com account. Just use the URL provided in this book to view the free tools that are available for it. Then, click on the "download" button for the free tool you want, and follow the prompts that appear to log in to your NewHarbinger.com account and download the material.

You can also save the free tools for this book to your **Free Tools Library** so you can access them again anytime, just by logging in to your account! Just look for this button on the book's free tools page. ➜ **+ Save this to my free tools library**

If you need help accessing or downloading free tools, visit **newharbinger.com/faq** or contact us at **customerservice@newharbinger.com**.